MAKING LOVE WITH THE LAND

MAKING LOVE WITH THE LAND

ESSAYS

JOSHUA WHITEHEAD

UNIVERSITY OF MINNESOTA PRESS
MINNEAPOLIS

Published by the University of Minnesota Press
111 Third Avenue South, Suite 290
Minneapolis, MN 55401-2520
http://www.upress.umn.edu

ISBN 978-1-5179-1447-9 (hc)

A Cataloging-in-Publication record for this book is available from the Library of Congress.

Printed in the United States of America on acid-free paper

The University of Minnesota is an equal-opportunity educator and employer.

31 30 29 28 27 26 25 24 23 22   10 9 8 7 6 5 4 3 2 1

For Dustin.
And for every person who has touched profound pain.

If you or anyone you know is in immediate crisis, please call the National Suicide Prevention Lifeline at 1-800-273-TALK.

"By the way, I forgive you."

—Brandi Carlile, *By the Way, I Forgive You*

"No one asked this of me, but I wanted to keep watch of the dying everywhere, so I could figure out how to care for a bleeding sentence."

—Billy-Ray Belcourt, *A History of My Brief Body*

"Borrowed time and borrowed world and borrowed eyes with which to sorrow it."

—Cormac McCarthy, *The Road*

Who Names the Rez Dog *Rez?*

I AM READING Ocean Vuong's *On Earth We're Briefly Gorgeous* and I let the words find me because the body always knows better than the mind does; muscles remember, they witness, like trees, riddles etch disease, and I am weeping willow, crying seeds and dripping saline from my hair (this is how I got my name, y'know?). Or consider how the cambiums of trees will warp a bullet civilly, make room for the wound in the structure of their being, crown themselves with flora—and I am singing starling. Ocean asks me, "Who will be lost in the story we tell ourselves? Who will be lost in ourselves? A story, after all, is a kind of swallowing." Feel the roots of me, an ecosystem of pain—I am anthropic in the desert of my being. Do you feel how much the winds have dried my tendrils? Feed me, water me, nurture me. I would be lying if I didn't say I too want to swallow you in this story I call essay, essay I call livelihood, life I pretend to call my own. I dog-ear Ocean's page and make an animal of story, I am looking for a wilderness in the act of being wild; I, here, a rez dog. I haven't seen you in a dog's age, by which I mean I haven't seen myself in years.

I am sitting on the hills of Dover, a space I rely on too heavily these days; the afternoon sun licking my shoulders, masseuse to the marks that stretch from the child-me who still fits inside me, and I have only just begun to find him again—that wild ancestral dream. People walk past me, staring: there I sit alone, barefoot, feet stroking the prairie grass and thistles, pricks not knowing the width of my soles. I cannot be harmed in this moment, by which I mean, I cannot afford to be. I puff a cigarette, curtail the smoke around the width of my neck, which remembers the lace of fingers around it—a finger trap, a gag toy. I let the smoke burn away the oils of your pads, which seed deep into me. I listen to Maggie Rogers's "Back in My Body" on repeat, tilting my cheeks to the sun, let pîsim kiss them into roses and I am blooming flower; you, a shrike to my stamens. I hold myself as if I were a babe, bare legs with thin hairs wrapped up into my chest: I, a papoose. As for those who stop and gawk at a lone NDN sitting in the long grass, the other "you" of this story texts me: "They're just stunned by your beauty in the sun." I tell you that if they are, it's entirely for me

today—I am majesty and my body is a living cornucopia. I eat
my own seeds—which isn't to say I consume myself, for once,
but rather that I wilt my pain into nutrient, and I am ourobo-
ric. My hair, which I model on Steve Harrington, flails in the
wind, to the point where I look Medusan in this Mohkinstsis
light. I look at the "you's" who have harmed me in ways big
or small, and I will you all to stone, carry you like gall in the
bladder of my being and expunge you in the beautiful delight
of a well-deserved urination. I am a body not needing to be
owned. Instead, I am owed, and no man can consume, let
alone hold, my plurality in this zipper I call a body. Or maybe
I mean to say that here, in this field, hair a zephyr of raze, I
become âtim, dog, relinquished from the prison-house of the
now, and I bark horror back into that doghouse while I rest
among the multitudes.

I am a rez dog in this moment, a vicious sight.

I read reports of rez dogs, of how moniyâw come to steal
them, beef jerky in hand, lure them into a car and drive off to
transplant them into suburbia. I think of my three sisters,
who have been thrown into a pot of soup. I am looking for
them; have you eaten? I imagine those rez dogs strapped in the
back seat of a Volvo watching the horizon recede, and their
found family howling into the night, "Heck, where are you?"
In this vignette, I am the rez dog and you are the driver, and it's
a hot July evening during the Calgary Stampede. The window-
panes sweat, and my tongue is panting for moisture. My skin
aches to be touched, but, like a frog's, it weeps when you lay a

hand upon my back. You grab me by the leash you have locked around my neck, force me close, my whiskers receding from your rank breath, your tongue the scent of fermentation, and I, my own muzzle. You promise me companionship and I bow to your feigned generosity, if only because the skyline is a dark ring and tipîskâw pîsim cannot see me here. Already, I am strategizing survivability amongst the abandoned buildings, looming like spectres in the peripheries of my vision because I am trained to stare at you. Hand tightened around my collar, you bring yourself into me with the force of a bookbinder—even this assemblage of sound drips with violence and I am wet with ink. When you are done, you promise me a home, in its largest connotations, and I reassemble done as doom, home being a torture chamber, a cage, kennel, the terrible weight of pounds. Your body expunged, you smile a gluttonous grin, and I paw the door of your vehicle, escape into the night. I am feral in this delight, having returned from the throes of entrapment and survived, fleeing into the safety of a transformed me. I enter the vomitorium of who I am and hack up severance, lick the salty rue clean to chew the bone of you. I howl for my kin, who rush to my side. Don't underestimate me, wendigo, I have chewed larger men than you into dust, blown through monuments, pissed on flagships, and you are only six inches of a man pretending he is ten. Together, a pack, we crush bone into fracture, crunch calcium into slop, will you the smiling death, a sudden syndrome, that slow necrosis.

"Just deadly," we will say. And I will stop in my routine, sit, and ask: Why do we use "deadly" to describe achievement or self-esteem, why must we entomb NDN success through the verbosity of death? I don't say that to my pack, though, because I don't want to question those who continually save me, even if they can sometimes damn me. My kin bring me back to the rez, and we settle into the long prairie grass, cuddle in a ball of fur and dust, mouths salivating a river of froth. They lick my ducts with tongues sanded into soft leather, nuzzle noses into one another, sleep side by side: this is how a rez dog survives.

The circularity of the second person chokes me: Who is the you I am addressing? And I would be lying if I didn't say: I have missed you forever. My, you're a shapeshifter, m'boy— or am I the one who shifts? Here, in my bed, beneath fairy lights and vinework, I am beside a you whose chest blazes with similar glory, patch of spirit, bed of dandelion, and I am grazing softly, regurgitant—is this you "you" in my bedsheets when I pool between his thighs?

I am only making love to myself, aren't I?

What does loneliness mean to a rez dog whose foot is wounded from a trapper's coils? Look around you, my ancestors will say, at the vastness of what you call living, watch where your skin flakes off in the wind and thins into a feeding, where a hair follicle stems into a dandelion, sweat a sweet drink. Loneliness, they'll say, is a mode of being dejected, not from relations, for those are plentiful and you are hungry, but from the act of rejecting that which is honest. Honesty, they'll say, is all around you, and these are the relations that detect rejection. Look to the purple heads, honesty, *Lunaria annua*, those silver coins that rattle in the wind—ecology is its own economic. Honesty, that beautiful flower, whose roots look like fingers in the soil—coil yourself into it, stem into cell, finger the wet mud, and reach down into the earth of me. Do you see "you" there? Storage roots are a network of hyperlinks, and I am out of time: you are perennial, and this concept you call temporality is an orality. I tell you, I am looking for the pup in me, the one that knew no shame. And I look at my stomach, my arms, my shoulders, see the clawings of a pup too rough with its mother. I am valiant in my ferality, by which I mean I am no longer that rez dog. Rather, I am the one removed from the servitude of civility and I return to the hinterland of who I am: child-me, elder-me, present-me all dancing vigorous round steps in this pit I call pimatisowin, the act of living. I love the me I become in orality. It's just—why can't I bring that into being beyond this page? I am in retrograde, and this essay is an act of all the things I've been mourning to tell you.

Don't expect too much from me, for I am slowly dying, and you have paid to witness this.

In this escape act of an essay, I have enacted and endured. I hear "everyone around me [is] saying you should be so happy now" in my AirPods, as Maggie Rogers wails in "Light On," and yet I, a daisy of a man, am continually attracted to the light of you, that second-person address. The other "you's" of this story eat from the palm of me, like a canker, worm, maple, the hardwood of my structuring. I am blown righteous with holes, here, in this moment: See the indents stitching together the orality of my temporariness? I think about how much I have given in this history: I see how much I have soaked into your floorboards and the zigzag stitches of your clothes that present your chest hair like a bouquet. But when I go into the tomb of the history that is mine, I see nothing of you save for a gallery of nail holes all screaming "fill me, filmme, filiusme."

I pace my home for hours on end, alone, listening to Rufus Wainwright's "Dinner at Eight," waiting to hear the wail of you from across the lot so I can know that I too held some type of significance in the life you are now living. I find a stone I saved from a tender moment we once shared, a memento, one I plucked from Bow sîpîy, all ruddy and smoothed from the rocking soliloquy of its mother and all her aunties. And in my maddened haze, I strike it against my abalone, casket of medicine, hearse of mindfulness, I am trying to spark a fire and become holy in the smoke—I am begging Creator to make me well again because I am weakened in this state and the root of me, the only face that smiles these days, aches to be dead-eyed into a shroud that will rig me into rigour, make me red sky. And yet, I am also striking this flint with instruction from Rufus, to break this pronominal form, this "you," down into its roots too, inspect "you" elementally, granite of loss, determine not its ecological but its emotional value to me. Instead, I break me, because this "you" is a simulation, and I am faced with truth.

And ain't that the funniest thing about writing? The "you" I keep invoking is multifarious, shattered glass, and I have only ever been talking to myself. Instead, when I go to the old home, I sit amongst the rez dogs, all kibble breath and piss dribble, ask them for companionship, conceptualize rez dogs as teacher, rez dogs as sacred, rez dogs as the greatest promise of the future through the metaphor of their bodies, their stories, their tattered pelts and crooked teeth in the apocalyptic followings that we are stalking. And I am here, looking for the good home, both in their skins and in my own—and I echo starling about it now.

My Body
Is a Hinterland

SOMETIMES I DREAD the evening, knowing that my mind will wrap itself around my body like a straitjacket and make me experience every bit of every painful thing I have ever endured. I watch movies at night, a combination of green tea and melatonin dissolving beneath the tongue while I wait for the inevitable. I whirl shards of hormones around and through my frenulum webbing, a mucosa that hearkens me back to my gestational days—I've had this tongue for over 1,500 weeks now. I lie on my side, head propped on my arm for so long that when I get up, my head wants to roll off my neck. Sometimes I let it do that, and I sit with myself beheaded, by which I mean bereaved, spilling out the only things I ate that day: spiders and anxiety knotted together like a muscle scratching on the floor. I fall asleep like this and wake up curled into myself, knowing only the word "circumference" in the morning. Melatonin takes away my memories of the evening; I wake up, not knowing if I've slept or if a dream was real, or if all life is a hunt for GABA. I know the night happened only by these signs: there are feathers in the carpet and a pillow with a concave, like a contact lens. I can never fully see if I'm the feather or the wool.

I sometimes sleep long after the world has fallen asleep, and wake before it rubs the crust from its ducts. I go out onto my patio, light up a cigarette, stare into my courtyard. The felines are awake at this time, caged predators pondering their own wilderness. What are we both hunting for right here, right now, my kin? I look at mistik, heavy with kôna, weighted down by whiteness in the bough, in the break. I blow a kiss to mistik and think of our mistikwânak, think of what is running through us. Do we meet here in our fibre, in the mornings, when we relieve ourselves? Pulp, poison, oxygen, dioxide. Our cores are rings that show our age; mine come from crows who flock to my eyes, yours from the exhalations I give. I giggle to myself, exult in our celebrations. We both consume that which kills us, and rise triumphant in wâpan, both still waiting for pîsim.

Sometimes I leave my apartment during the day to walk out into Valleyview. I found mahkêsîs there once, far from her den, which is marked by a Hydro stick with an orange plastic flag wrapped around it. She frolicked in the long grasses and made me follow her to the edge of the hill—and there, between serrated blades of maskosiy, was a vaudeville show of red, orange, and white. mahkêsîs carries autumn on her back, carries sunsets, embodies time. When I reach the edge, I see all of Mohkinstsis splashed against the coral of daylight, I see the erections of banks and telephone companies cutting into the sunlight, I see the Bow, miwasin sîpiy, wrapped around it like a corsage, I see the Rocky wacîyawak wavering, by which I mean waving, in the humidity—heck, even old mosôm with all his rickety bones has learned how to bend and not break.

During the height of my insomnia, I found myself continually dreaming of mahkêsîs. She runs through my dreamscapes like a guide, or a waypoint. I begin to see her in real life too, darting across the dusty prairie roads of Manitoba late at night, lit by headlight and glaring eye. I see her on the hills of Calgary, in ditches and dens. And then I see her in Saskatoon—here I am dreaming—and she is leading me through the Woodlawn Cemetery where my grandmother is buried. I have been here many times during what I call my mourning pilgrimages—disheartened at my grandmother's lack of headstone and instead relying on the iCemetery app to find her in this labyrinth of baroque decor. In the dream, mahkêsîs leads me by running ahead and looking back, like an expectant pup, until we are both standing over the grave. The wind is rough, my hair is longer now, my face aged, and even mahkêsîs carries the gait of time. We conduct our annual mourning ceremonies by digging up handfuls of earth, placing new sweetgrass braids and rose petals in the hole, and covering over the wound with hand and paw, nail and talon. Whose hand is mine in this first-person experience? Am I fox or human? When I come to, I feel rejuvenated, afresh for the first time in ages after little to no sleep. I call my mother up immediately—it's now afternoon for both of us, me in Calgary, Alberta; her in Selkirk, Manitoba—and tell her of the dream. She halts me partway towards my narrative finale, says, "Shut up!" in the playful way that NDN women inhabit, and orates, "You won't believe this, but a fox just weaved through our yard just now." We share this serendipity across the prairies, in different spaces but in the same emotive states. And in this cacophonous crying in prayer and ceremony for help, I find you, mahkêsîs—by which, perhaps, I mean nohkôm—waving me into a refuge waived of the world's hurtful temperaments.

Sometimes I tell myself I'd slice a skyscraper in half and swallow it whole—vats of magnesium breaking down the highways in my gut that block the transmission of neurons that calm and hold me when I need this. My belly is full of quantum physics, elements making love to one another—metals plate organs, earth meets water, and at the atomic level, I am a kind of biotech. My belly is a prairie, my belly is the bush, my belly is a wild land, hinterland, ancestral land.

I find nikâwiy at the core.

I eat wild meat, I eat raw; I find the taste of domesticity a lack, the taste of game a kind of feral excess. nohtâwiy and nocâwis took me hunting once. We hunted apisimôsos but instead found maskwa squatting in a bush. When they handed me the rifle, my knees buckled and my body sweated out all of its medicines. I refused, and they took the rifle back and told me to go and wait in the truck up the hill. There was child-me in the back seat of a Ford pickup, covering his ears and holding his gut, in a full-on fetal position. What does it mean to be fetal? nohkôm told me that a fetus is an embryo, that we begin at the end as the proto-organ of the body: the anus. nohtâwiy tells me of nocâwis and nikâwîs all hunting on their trapline—everyone afraid to run into a bear on their hunt for pelts and venison. nohtâwiy and nocâwis hide in the bush while nikâwîs squats behind a tree to defecate. When she returns, they growl out of sight, rushing in on her on all fours, looking like two hunched bears, these nêhiyaw nâpewak regressing into a state of play. nikâwîs screams, runs full tilt toward their truck with her pants down, feces splattering in her footfalls, while nohtâwiy and nocâwis burst into laughter. Her angry approach towards them bearlike in itself, hand cupped into a hammer, which loosens and falls as she buckles over into laughter. I think of nanabush and nanaboozho here, the tricksters of our peoplehoods, of their ability to remove genital and organ, to be a talking head, a moving penis, a quacking anus—and here, three adult nêhiyâwak regressing into children again upon the earth that birthed them, laughing at fecal jokes and bare asses, unbothered by their nudity or shame, and cackling like ravens right there on their hunting ground.

Even through the scrunch of cartilage, the blockage of a canal, I heard the bang of the rifle and the whimper of a wildness defeated. They called out to me to help put tobacco out for maskwa, to offer thanks for the giving, and they skinned maskwa there and then. nohkôm makes bear grease from its essential oils, its fat, rubs it in her hair, tells herself that it will help with her balding. I remember wondering: Do you need to smell like death to ferment life? When I ate maskwa, I felt him stirring in the belly—as if maskwa had transplanted himself into me. On a bio-organic level, I dance with maskwa, make love to maskwa. As he churns in the gut, I am nourished and alive. The material maskwa breaks down into a series of amino acids and minerals, and becomes my body's lactic acids, its own enzymes and sugars. I like to think that we meet there in the navel, that bow of skin, that severed place, my first mouth. I pretend it's a flower bed, his amino acids and my body-milk coming together as syllabic elements, and share a kiss that can only be heard as onomatopoeia. There he is in the muscle when it extends, and he eats at me to build me; there he is in the sweat pulsing from skin, and he feeds me to exhaust me; and there he is in excrement, like a symbol, or a tobacco offering, thanking me for giving myself. Maybe that's why we're cousin-kin—because in the end we both decompose into oil; we both meet in the organs. To kiss an element, or to kiss on the elemental level, is a type of coupling—the quantum physics of all kinship structures. To bind oxygen

with hydrogen makes a covalent bond, is a sharing of elec-
trons. To move inwards is a type of microscopic embodiment.
To move inwards, I begin to think more and more, is less
abstraction and more concretization. What happens on the
body happens inside it first.

When they say I am a "savage" for eating dried or wild meat,
I think of "sauvage." As much as I want to word-associate that
into a good smoked deer sausage, I eat the word whole and dissolve it in saliva. When the word crumbles in on itself, which
English far too easily does, I churn it like butter in my intestines. "Sauvage" has a gamy taste on the tongue, like maskwa—
so much so that I wonder if those settlers too have eaten wild?
The lower intestine squeezes it into silvaticus, and I still taste
you on my tongue. Silva meets my flora and becomes reunited
with its peoples as my bacterium comes to greet it, offers yeast
and bannock lard. Even as we become nothing, meaning that
which cannot be named, meaning an embodiment beyond an
English understanding, we become all-things, we become kin
on a microscopic, hypermetropic, multiplicitous level. Saliva
meets silva, meaning forest-dweller, and we move again to the
hinterland, the place beyond the forest, so that when I defecate
I originate—I give back to those who gave to me. The belly is
a world maker, is a Fourth world, is my ancestral grounds.

THESE DAYS I LIE awake next to nîcimos, who sleeps like a
babe beside me, all nestled in his body hairs and neatly folded
on his side of the bed. I let the melatonin melt in my webbing

and become an economic, which really means I think of home. When people ask me about Manitoba, I complain about the extreme cold and the extreme heat—Manitoba is a testament to adaptability. I think of Gimli, that old Icelandic beach town, and how we braved the waters in order to swim in Lake Winnipeg, a lake full of E. coli.

nîcimos and I visited Gimli when he first visited Manitoba in 2018. He is Scandinavian, and I wanted to show him there is space for him in Treaty 1. We walked the pier and looked at the yachts and boats. We surveyed the art lining the seawalls, which has been there since 1997. A lone buffalo has always stood out for me. Many of the other paintings have been restored into a new glory, Icelandic or Viking, artistic footprints of settler portraits touched up and brought into modernity; but the buffalo and her calf have mossed into sediment. The lake likes to eat paint, as do the seagulls overhead who shit on murals and fly off cackling, and the rising humidity salts and scrubs the stone clean. But the buffalo continues to stare at the yachts, as if perplexed—she in all her decadence, with every hue of brown and red rotating on her skin. The sky behind her is a baby blue, and it meets her calf halfway, fluffed up with clouds that contour the sky then blend into a gradient. Their background is the prairies, evergreens, pines, willows all shim-mying on the horizon.

Sometimes I think of this beach town when I try to sleep—the way the sand will burn the soles of your feet if it's a too-too hot day in July, or the way the wind pelts your skin with sand but kisses any injuries, the way those orange tube-slides skid your bottom and toss you into the sand, all laughter and toothy smiles. I think of the whimsy I used to attribute to this beach town as a child, the way it lit up like a strip, all noise and bottle-clanking; I think of the pathway into the water and how it was always littered with stones that bruised your toes, how the beach would foam and lather the ground it rested upon, how the water table would sometimes cascade into a deep hole that would topple you over and plunge you into its cavity, how nîtisân and I would sit along the shore and let the waves knock us back, over and over again. She is now a very beautiful woman, nîtisân, but when the waves slicked her hair back and her mouth was half-full of baby yet, when her dimples held water like buckets, and when her laugh could choke the world into a moment of silence—those are my favourite moments of her.

Tonight, when I think of Gimli, here at 3 a.m. in my bed, I think of the pub where nîcimos and I went on that day I took him there, the Ship and Plough with its rainbow flag tacked squarely into a corner. We sat, both a sweaty mess, and ordered a round of beer and raised our glasses in a silent but loving way. Beside us sat a group of men, a mixture of younger and older, discussing transgender peoples and mocking Caitlyn Jenner. Funny how quickly a reprieve can be stolen right out from under you. But we knew how to perform the pageant of passing, knew how to move our bodies, how to cough correctly, how to fold the arms, how to breathe, how to inflect the voice and laugh, how to look at one another. We spoke like telepaths, both knowing the other's body could betray itself in a small gesture and inform on the other—body like a code, knuckles wrapping taps.

I got up to ask our waitress to cancel our next round, said that we'd like to pay and kindly leave. Returning to my seat, I heard the men's voices grow louder, more boisterous, filling the room like a miasma, speaking in thick tones that gagged us with their viscosity. Waiting for the waitress felt like a lifetime in such a small bar. When she brought the bill, we quickly paid and gathered our things to leave, the town now a maw that wanted to swallow us whole. The men's conversation had changed to reconciliation. When I looked back one final time, the word "savage" poured out of their mouths, and in my haste to leave, whipping my head back around to its rightful nook, I swear their heads spun around and the word "savage" stuck to my skin. This savage hailing far from my playful ruminations on the gamy taste of "sauvage" cuisines. Sometimes I think the lake in that town exists at the bottom of the world, the watershed draining from the Rocky Mountains, from South Dakota, through to northern Ontario. nîcimos, his heavy hands chipped from farm labour, pulled me into the car and we looked at one another with a desperation that erupted into laughter. It's funny how a threat can become a treat sometimes. But I still churned that word around in the mouth, like a forkful of gristle that refused to be swallowed: savage, sauvage, all foreign and peppered beyond taste or sense upon the game-fed tongue of my mouth.

They say Gimli is poisoned by E. coli, not because of runoff from farms within the watershed but because of the birds that flock from the nearby marshlands—the geese and gulls. To remedy this, the town installed a fake eagle on the beach in order to scare away the birds that flock here to feast on food scraps, garbage, and minnows left by fishermen. Their shit stains the water, they say, their feces plummeting back onto shore and leaching down into the sand, creating a cesspool reservoir. I think of my body like that reservoir, riddled with stains from words like "savage" and "faggot." All that waste coagulates into a mound of defecation that clumps together like a mutated body, one that poisons its host, one that cries to be expunged. I sometimes imagine the waste of me deep down in the belly, thrashing against the lining there because I haven't eaten fibre, due in part to a lack of funds, allowing me to afford only scraps. It gurgles in its acidic bath, doggy-paddling to beat hell, and when it doesn't get its way, it bulks together until it hulks, immobile, dying, throwing neurotoxins into the blood and through the skin. It raises the temperature of the body, makes the flesh bubble salt water, dilutes the pigmentation of skin so that I look like milk walking in the daylight. My mouth dries, becomes sticky, and all thoughts regarding my well-being become a feverish flourishing. I think of the lake as I would myself, I think of Manitoba as I would myself, I think of the world as I would myself—and rename myself Doomsday. How does a minnow's head, when digested through a gull's gizzard, cause a heat wave across the world? How does that in turn divine ruination for the boreal? How do the grill marks on a steak spell doom for the caribou? And just when did I become the apocalypse?

When I'm on the Gimli beach, I look for that eagle, all stoic in its plasticity, and imagine that the birds own this land. I think of the plastic eagle as I would a frog prince; his wings are erect and his beak is a down-turned, well-proportioned appendage. I think about climbing onto his perch, crossing my legs beneath his talons, and kissing the tip of that rostrum. I imagine him reeling to life with a rallying cry, tearing into my back and pulling out the wings that have always been there, and tossing me upwards into the sky. I'd see a convocation of eagles flying overhead and all the birds coming together to let go a collective defecation and purge ourselves of our standstill—a flurry of white shit to enhance that hue of whiteness below. The lake would clap and recede, it would spell out "Fuck Off" in the sand and retreat into its bottom—all mamas need rest, to bathe and lick their wounds, and the lake deserves one too. And off we'd fly, into their eagle eyrie beyond the horizon of water. Home, here I come again, I say; sauvage is a grove, not a grave.

I WIELD, AS I CALL IT, my mutant ability, an uncanny gift I've always had to energize myself on the edge of exhaustion. This is a tool I have used to survive the combined workloads of grad school, touring, writing, teaching, my social life, and travelling. "Oh, I got three hours of sleep last night? That's okay, I can work until two in the morning," is a refrain I often announce to the world. I've felt how this coping mechanism has drained every molecule of energy my body can house. This, combined with my insomnia, has left me a shell of a man many a night. A kin of mine once told me during a conversation not to "abuse my gifts" and this has been a lesson I've held on to ever since.

What does it mean to abuse a gift? Can these abilities I have to work into the bone hours of the evening and wake in the dew of new morning be bruised, tattered, cut? Can I abuse writing? Surely in the project of this agenda we call "literature" a person—especially one who is queer and/or BIPOC—can be asked to exchange the body for an economy, to work calorically as a means of currency, to burn the midnight oil so as to continue the project of pipelines that fund the very root of this institution. Here, this abuse I inflict willingly upon myself is a means of bloodletting into a vial, the blood then aged, like a fine wine, until it too becomes fossilized fuel running the larger machines of Canada, intricate cogs pressing through the coagulation of clogs, and I am celebrated for showing the body in its scraped, raped glories—all of this within the voyeurism of a genre we call non-fiction. Then again, I don't think that everything is a simple binary, and that to expend oneself means gifting one's inheritance. For surely writing, and this is my aim, empowers, uplifts, and grants representation to those communities of which I am a part. I wonder, then, what is the "gift" of insomnia—if it can be called such a thing?

I sometimes joke in writing residencies and workshops that in order to best embody a character, fictional or poetic, we must treat them as if they are a vessel and we the actor, they the syllabic, we the animator; and we must method-act ourselves into their bodies. What I mean by this is what I have come to understand as the "gift" of insomnia: I sleep with my characters. During episodes when I lie awake or am overcome with thoughts that ache to take centre stage in the anxious hierarchy of my mind's agenda, I place characters in the spotlight, survey them sensually: How do they smell? If I were to kiss them, what would their tongue taste like? What of the perfumes of their body odours? What does their skin feel like after it begins to shed from sunburn? What rhythms do their vernaculars sing? I wilt into the rot of sleep with these characters beside, atop, or within me. I hold tightly to them, I dream of them, often *as* them, and am opened into new world views, insights, and/or emotional states. I conducted this exercise many times with Jonny, especially as I finished writing him at a writing studio in the mountains. I willed him to spoon me in the wee hours of the night and dreamed languidly of his daydreams, desires, kinks, loves. We need to make our stories animate beings, we need to place them into oratories of history and of futurity. We need to conceptualize our fantastical dreams as very real decolonized futures.

I am often asked about where I write, and how I write—a question that has perplexed me for years, even as I have tried to sound like what we might call a "real writer" in the landscape of literature. I wish it were as easy for me to announce that my writing praxis was done in the sanctuary of a café, coffee in hand, mind alit with beautiful narrative—but my writing spaces are not so ordinary. I spend an ornate amount of time writing in bed, splayed on my stomach in the fevered hours of the evening or wee hours of the morning, stitching thoughts, images, affects, and conversations into a quilt of baroque textures. For me, then, the bedroom becomes a space ripe with possibility, a type of shared intimacy and vulnerability between myself and those I house like lovers spooned into vertebrae.

HERE IN THE BONE hour of dusk, I'll transfix myself atop my own star blanket, spilling like a cup of water held in weaved basketry. I have been attuned to my dreams since I was a child. Here I have dreamed of the dead; here, as a toddler, I recalled to my parents, with vivid memory, my great-grandfather and -uncles who passed before I was born. I have had dream premonitions as an adolescent too, of cousins rapt by the Red, of helices mutating from the carcinogen in my father. I have dreamed of apocalypse, doom, overwhelming noise, and silent destructions for as long as I can recall—dreams that repeat, visiting me frequently, that play themselves like trilogies, willing themselves into continuation even as I awake and refresh between these episodes.

If insomnia is gift, a tinkering as I have said, in what ways is a dream like a video game, a virtual reality? And if such virtual realities instruct us, and we embody ourselves as avatars, do they mend us? During my time at a writers' retreat in the mountains, I had a conversation with the writer Canisia Lubrin about dreams. She told me that lately she'd been having intense dreams, prophetic almost, and we agreed this is a story many of us share in the current ecological and political end-times climate of the globe. I am plagued by nightmares when I am able to sleep—and I've taken to swigging NyQuil as a remedy. I feel as if I am reaching out to this voidless "you" in order to say, help me, by which I must mean: help us.

My father once asked a medicine woman, Lillian, what I should do about my childhood dreaming. "Does he fly in his dreams?" she asked, to which my father nodded, and she responded, "Tell him simply to witness—only the storytellers fly in dream." I say this not to romanticize what I do, but to say that it has become my practice to witness and interpret what I think of as ancestral knowledge in the form of this act we call "dreaming." It's there that I write, in that realm of deep REM; and I speculate, as many people do, that "dreaming is a form of preparing for future threats." What better way to fore-warn about the machinery of colonialism than in the animated cooing of such dreams; and what better way to foreground the emergence of joy in the bridge between loss and becoming?

As I dream, my bed becomes a knob between worlds—the ledge upon which I perch to witness.

I have this recurring dream, one that happens many times a year, especially in times of extreme stress. My body, in its breathing, knows when it is coming, and as I lull into sleep, I prepare. The dream features me standing on a grid of pixels and glowing linework, much like the background of the film

Tron, and in the middle of the grid sits a sphere that continually widens in this limited space. I move towards the edge of this digital world as the sphere expands, filling my hearing with increasing volumes of intersecting voices and electrical hissing until it becomes unbearable to stand without clutching my ears. As this sphere balloons to the point of threatening to knock me off the skirting of this world, the collective sound now a deafening screech, I focus on one voice, a guide in some semblance, and pound meaning into this soundscape. This is when I fall—but am caught and held by oratories, and I wake into newer resolutions, brighter revolutions. The dream teaches me to listen, and listen fiercely, to focus on what is pleading to be heard, crying in unison, and to engage. Readers of my work might remember some of these ruminations in *full-metal indigiqueer*: dreams of automatons and atomic apexes, of saviours armoured in codex and machinery. Or may remember, in *Jonny Appleseed*, Jonny's raptured *The Day after Tomorrow* orca-crying tsunami nightmare—one I share continually with him; or his bear-topping scene, a dream I too had while finishing the manuscript in the mountains.

As a child, I was horrifically obsessed with those tabloid magazines in the checkout lines of our local grocery store, Gaynor's Family Foods. As my mom would ring through groceries, I'd survey these publications: *Sun Magazine*, *Weekly World News*, and the *Enquirer*. Often they'd have hilarious headlines such as HILLARY CLINTON ADOPTS ALIEN BABY; BIGFOOT DIET!: HE LOSES 150LBS—IT CAN WORK FOR YOU

TOO; and MINI-MERMAID FOUND IN TUNA SANDWICH. Though, more often than not, these magazines sensationalized apocalypse, reading, IS THIS THE END OF THE WORLD?; THE FINAL DAYS: ARMAGEDDON; and THE ANTI-CHRIST IS ALIVE— AND LIVING IN THE US. As an adult, surveying child-me, my fascination with and hyperbolic fear of "the end" blossomed through these readings and of course the heightened cultural moments of Y2K—a day in which I sincerely thought the world would end through atomic warfare—and the purported doomsday of 2012. Even outside the supermarket, I was bombarded by doom. Jehovah's Witnesses would hand out copies of the *Watchtower* and *Awake!* to me as I walked to school, with their headlines of DEATH: IS IT REALLY THE END? and ARMAGEDDON: WHAT IS IT? WHEN WILL IT COME? accompanied by terrifying images of disaster painted in a Rockwellian fashion. I'm tickled by the irony now, as a Two-Spirit Indigenous person, that I was afraid of the apocalypse—for surely we have already survived "finality" and have moved into a post-dystopian future that shimmers on the edge of Canada's utopian vision of itself in the contemporary. And I too, like my fellow writer Canisia Lubrin, have been so plagued by dreams, mostly recurring nightmares, that I must ask: What do I/we dream of when the world is on the brink of obliteration? Is insomnia not a by-product of a world moving towards its end-stop? And how do I, and we, as disenfranchised folks, use such dreams? I place a desperate but necessary emphasis on the root of this word, "obliteration," and huff it into orality.

My ideal writing space, then, is in dreams and bedrooms—
me the bent recorder between kissing worlds, wanting to be
heard and touched. Here I'll lie until dawn, possessed by the
need to spill, forgetting even to eat or drink or urinate until
I feel the portrait of what I've witnessed is written into pliabil-
ity, plausibility. Here I'll listen to classical music to stimulate
my thoughts—attuned to the contemporary queer classic
reimaginings of Darren Creech and Cris Derksen, feral on key
and string—and sing into being the messaging and warn-
ings and love-coos and death-hymns of that which I witness in
the night only to rinse off in the pupa of morning.

I have been summoning my fictional protagonist Jonny
into the dreamscapes of my mind for the past ten years. And
he is a character I have come to know intimately, from chicken-
pox forehead scar to foreskin to the loop of pubic hair painted
onto his toenail. This is what insomnia and dreaming has
gifted me. Although I wrote Jonny, I have been astounded by
the excitement over, and requests for me to read, the "maskwa
topping" scene wherein Jonny bottoms for a bear in the mountains of Alberta. There are many dream sequences within *Jonny
Appleseed* that, during the writing and editing processes, I was
asked to remove because they distracted from the "realism" of
the novel; Indigenous epistemologies were being meagrely
read as "magic realism" and thereby as folk tale, mythology, or
fantastical. Surely, they can be, but I held steadfast to keeping
those dream sequences. They are, in my opinion, the "realist"
senses of Jonny's world as compared with the hellish "reality"

he inhabits as a queer-femme-Indigenous nâpew. As I have been taught, dreams are fundamental to my Indigenous knowledge base(s) or epistemologies; to many others, they work as systems of instruction. They instruct us as we embody ourselves or others as avatars; they mend us, heal us, warn and rejuvenate us.

I am reminded here of nohtâwiy, a man who has survived cancer, a kidney removal, three major heart attacks, diabetes, government day schools, homelessness, substance addiction, and abuse. While my father was weighted down with cancer, he was working as a handyman for Ikwe-Widdjiitiwin, a shelter for women and their children who have fled or survived domestic abuse—a non-profit organization that my mother and grandmother had worked with for over twenty years. While there, my parents and grandmother met Lillian, an Ojibwe medicine woman who was an elder and adviser for the shelter. They quickly became fast friends and spent many hours, both at work and outside it, together as kin, helpers, friends, and caretakers. My father was hospitalized for months on end with kidney cancer, an after-effect of his years of substance abuse as a teenager and young man surviving homelessness after stints of foster care, youth remand centres, and adoption agencies. I entirely blame colonization, and the machinations of the Sixties Scoop and Child and Family Services, for the aftermath of trauma my father waded through like a thick mucus miasma that blocked him from the gestational emergence into adulthood. When Western pharmaceuticals and medicines failed my father, we thought he was on his deathbed.

As a young teenager, I recall him lying on his bed, a skeleton compared with the full-figured Cree-Dené man I'd always known him to be, atop a faded green star blanket that had turned mint from overuse. I recall child-me looking at my father, his gaunt hand in the full pads of my fleshy, sweaty boy hands. His bones felt like daggers in my palms. I recall my mother and grandmother reassuring him that things would be fixed once we got a medicine woman to visit him—and saying they had called Lillian to visit.

Lillian, the most adamant of women, one who held the attention of a room even in the rickety bones of her Elderhood, arrived with a turtle rattle, sweetgrass, and various other medicines in her maskihkiywat. She instructed my sister and me to step into the basement and not to come upstairs until we were called upon. Both nîtisân and I retreated to my room in the basement of our rental home, holding each other desperately in the musky, damp air of my bedroom, listening eagerly to the voices just above us. We heard the constant jiggle of rattle and singing coming from the three women, imagining their held hands as triage around the bones of my father huddled on a ratty blanket. The chanting and rattling went on for what felt like hours, and in my child-memories the house shook, the air became as dense as a smudge, my ears became a stretched hide that thumped to the beat of wâpos outrunning and outsmarting mahihkân nôhcimihk—we heard maskwa roar above us, that deep guttural growl that grasped us, then loosened its fangs and split through the air like lightning.

My father's cancer went into remission a few months later, and when nitisân and I asked him about that evening, he was truthful with us, careful and gentle but awed and fearful simultaneously. "That woman, Lillian," he said, his hands upon both of our shoulders and his eyes milky, "she gave me bear medicine for the cancer, you probably smelled it, eh?"

We both looked at each other and nodded.

"She told me I would be visited by her helper, and they'd guide me through the healing," he announced, almost laughing, nearly crying, "and all I did was sleep and dream for days afterwards. Heck, though, one night I woke up in the middle of the night and I shot straight up, eh, Tina?" He looked to my mother for approval, and she giggled and nodded. "And I swear I heard a damned ol' bear just growling to beat hell beside me, spittle and everything." His grip tightened on our shoulders, though not to the point where it hurt us—just to make sure we were linked into his story, paying attention, listening fiercely. "And then I looked at the damn door, afraid to get off the bed in case he'd just rip my leg clean off. And that ol' door just opens, bright light and everything just shining on through it, like I was going to the goddamn Pearly Gates or something, and there's this man, or at least I think they're a man, long hair, ribbon skirt, bare chest, and feathers—everything. And that person walks up to me, places their hand on my shoulder, and just says, 'You'll heal, m'boy, you'll heal over the next few days, my friend here, maskwa, will be with you to rip the rot right out of you, so don't

be scared of him, all right? Just sleep and dream and you'll wake
into a day without the haze of sickness.'"

Such dreaming became a mending process, the body a newly
mended zipper able to hold its self together.

WHEN I RETURN to myself, it's 4 a.m., and I have been too far
away from myself. nîcimos is still sleeping. The sun will rise
soon, and my spirits are far too awake to rest now. I lie still,
I regulate my breath, I think of what an annoyance insomnia
is, because the body too quickly wants to turn itself over to
production, to exhaust itself and return to this space.

As the sun rises, I finally begin to tire. As I ready to sleep,
I know nîcimos will rise for work soon and I will be left to the
hauntings of an imagination that knows no rest. How easy it
is to write of places beyond ours, to word-craft a world into
being, when it's for others and not for the self. I lie down, mind
now finally exhausted to the point where it cries itself to sleep.
I close my eyes and think of savagery, tell myself that the mind
itself is a type of wilderness. As my mind prepares to hibernate,
I count time. I think: if 10 percent of the day is spent blinking,
and 30 to 40 percent dreaming, then we spend half our lives
inside ourselves. What does that mean, to spend half of our
lives inside?

I let my mind cocoon and turn myself over to the body, which
is to say the hinterlands. I feel as if I know the mind, which is
also to say the spirit, enough to call it a wilderness—but the
body, that I run from. The body is the area beyond. It jigs its legs

as I sleep, beating to a drum I can't yet hear. Still, there is a kindness in the unknown, a puzzle to decode, a webbing calling to be braided. I move there, thinking of maskwa, mahkêsîs, and kihîw; and let them all guide me to the nebula of these lands.

And there, in the middle, I always come across nikâwiy, waving me into the lodge.

I sit there, in the middle of me, and sweat until I disintegrate, until every ounce of fluid in the body—water, blood, semen, piss—purifies into a well. I become a lake, a watercourse, and drain, slowly, into the spirit-stream. nikâwiy teaches me how to be a spiritual mother, to give birth to the self for the self. "Lacus," I say, "sâkahikan"—which sounds so close to "sâkihitin." And in the wake I carry awasis into the blinding afternoon light. "Silvaticus," I say, "you are awasis tipêyimisowin pikwacaskîy, the wilderness I dream of."

Please don't lose you in the mourning.

On Ekphrasis
and Emphases

IN MY EARLIER DESIGNS as a writer, I learned to story-tell
through ekphrasis. In this I think I am like many writers who
have undertaken workshops only to look to painting for inspi-
ration. Because ekphrasis is a rhetorical exercise, one in which
an artist relates to another medium by describing its aesthetics,
form, or thematic essence, the act of ekphrasis is therefore one
of relations, a contract of kinships.

One of the first painters I ever sought to respond to was
William Kurelek, a Ukrainian-Canadian artist and writer
who often painted the prairies as embodying rather horrific
idyllic sensualities. Much of his work revolves around Manitoba,

primarily Stonewall, which is in the same Interlake district as my hometown, Selkirk. There are two paintings in particular that haunt me to this day: *This Is the Nemesis* and *When We Must Say Goodbye*. You, perhaps, may recognize some of these visual inspirations in my works. The earliest poems in my collection *full-metal indigiqueer* emerge from my fascination with the apocalypse and warfare and, in their chrysalis stages, were birthed in the atomic centre of Kurelek's nemesis, which can be seen huffing into a truffle on the horizon of his painting. In *When We Must Say Goodbye*, a lone woman sits on driftwood, staring sullenly at her feet in the centre of a wide-panning depiction of a beach at rest—a scene recalled in my novel *Jonny Appleseed*, where the titular character and his lover Tias survey each other's bodies and ponder the ethics of loving even while mourning for the ironic goodbye that will come between them.

I owe a great debt to Kurelek—but that verb, "owe," always cinches me. If ekphrasis is a relationship, then how do we navigate said kinship through the exchange of debt? How do I remunerate the painter? And how is debt like a tome—or, if considered through the lens of literature, through the desire to canonize, should I say tomb? I often play "find the hidden NDN" in art crafted upon Turtle Island—from Kurelek's *Indian Hitchhiking from Saskatchewan Series #2* through to the painting of "*e pluribus unum*,[1] mitakuye oyasin,[2]" in the horrific Netflix

---

[1] "out of many, one" the thirteen-letter traditional motto of the United States
[2] "all are related/relations" from Lakota linguistics

film about a cutthroat art critic, *Velvet Buzzsaw*. Then these relations become indebted, as Indigeneity within them becomes entombed, or surfaces for aesthetics while actual Indigenous peoples remain dislocated from the form of the artistry.

Recently, I watched *Spider-Man: Homecoming* and something caught my attention in the film's opening scene, which features Michael Keaton as the emergent antagonist, the Vulture, having a conversation with his ally Michael Chernus, a.k.a. the Tinkerer. They are holding a portrait of the Avengers drawn by a youth. "Things are never going to be the same now," narrates Keaton. "I mean, look at this, you got aliens, you got big green guys tearing down buildings. When I was a kid, I used to draw cowboys and Indians." He is quickly corrected by Chernus: "Actually, it's Native Americans." Keaton's character takes a brief reprieve to amusingly look at him before he asks, "Tell you what, though, it ain't bad, is it?" Chernus's character agrees, "No, yeah, kid's got a future," to the dismay of Keaton, "Yeah, well, we'll see I guess." I was drawn to this scene for its attempt at playfulness regarding Indigeneity, adolescence, and futurisms. The scene pans to the crumbling building of the Avengers Tower from the vantage point of a gentrified New York building. We then see Keaton's team excavating an alien structure that looks akin to a fossilized carcass, something that predates their arrival by some time, something Indigenous to its own land base and to its own world, a fossilized carcass that they dissect in order to create militarized bioweapons and nanotechnologies.

This scene rings too true to the current state of Indigeneity on Turtle Island, our literatures, and the buffering of an amalgamated Canadian canon. Literature as an augmentation is the decadence of anthropology, the end result(s) of excavation and its institutional grants, and the glamorized tales of fossil fuels and land/bodies made into literary technologies. I think of my young nêhiyâw cousin who watches these films religiously, who dresses up like these superheroes and aspires to be them through play and the imaginative. I think of Chris Hemsworth, the actor of the popularized Thor, who appropriated Indigeneity in order to "play Indian" during a Lone Ranger–themed party. I wonder what kind of mirrors are being crafted, and for whom? What is it that people think Indigeneity looks like? What is interpolated for them psychically when they swish that word around their mouths, when the syllables spring from their tongues? I think, that's *pale*-ontology: from cannibalizing the Huron to calling for a prize on how best to excavate/appropriate.

I take a cue from my Two-Spirit cybernetic trickster, Zoa, and learn to re-augment my body: transgressive, punk, Indigiqueer. I place myself into the film, Oji-Cree in NYC, and look up at that crumbling Avengers Tower in glee. I watch the structure come apart at its seams, laugh, think, "Yeah, that kid does have a future and you'll be the one to see." Tell those vultures, by which I mean wendigo, that they're colour-blind— that big green guy tearing down buildings is the mihko mistahâpêw, Red Hulk, tearing down structures and institutions.

If Indigeneity is a vanishing act, it's one we've perfected to ghost ourselves into the future, just ask Frenchie, Jared Martin, and all those Two-Spirit hero(in)es who learned to live and love beyond body, space, and time. Here I am attaching those loosened minerals to my skin to emerge a diamond-crusted NDN, full-metal and vicious in the light. I am not a whole thing, I am a web of fractures living in my brokenness; web like okimâw apihkêsîs, trickster spider who spun the original world-wide-web, all sticky with feeling and smooth as a weathered pebble.

Connection is a technology Indigeneity perfected.

I turn my eyes to Kent Monkman, a queer Cree painter whose drag alter ego Miss Chief often appears in his paintings. As a Two-Spirit Ojibwe-nêhiyaw femme-nâpew I energize myself in the ecosystems of Monkman's depictions. Often, in Monkman's paintings, we are shown a hyper-feminine Cree nâpew in lingerie, or draped with HBC blankets, in the downtown north end of Winnipeg or in parliament in Ottawa. *The Chase*[3] and *Seeing Red* are some of my favourite paintings because they call me into myself: someone who sees himself in the femininity of nêhiyaw ayâwin on the often hypermasculine and heteronormative streets of Winnipeg. I ask myself if I owe a debt to Monkman too—and, if so, how does that inform or rupture our relationship with each other?

---

[3] This painting was ultimately used as the cover of *full-metal indigiqueer*.

I identify as Two-Spirit, which means much more than simply my sexual preference within Western ways of knowing, but rather that I am queer, femme/iskwewayi, male/ nâpew, and situated this way in relation to my homelands and communities. I state this because queerness, or settler sexualities, has stolen so much from Two-Spiritedness—I am sovereign through what sovereignty calls me. Often, when I meander through an art gallery, I am overcome with feelings of obliteration—first, because I find that "hidden NDN" and remember that a museum is a scaffold that has executed relationality; and second, because I am bombarded by figures of femininity that bulge with boisterous beauty yet are beheaded in this catacomb. I find my femininity in fragments: here Mona Lisa's cheek on the floor, pinked with berry blush; here, pearl earrings and an earlobe sliced in half; here I come across the hem of a gold-leaf gown by accident; and here the sun hat of a woman distorted into disorder. And I wonder if what we consider the beauty of femininity is always laced with the sadistic. But I leave the cata-gallery feeling fulfilled because I too swell in the pubis, and here I am never asked to placate that largeness.

Maybe I tell you all this simply to ask: How am I in relation to myself? How am I indebted to my *self*? How do I subject myself to subjecthood? Perhaps I walk around an amalgamation, a symbiosis, of iconographies that I, myself, have Indigenized? Perhaps I am a nemesis, by which I mean the Greek *nemein*—or, giving what is due? How do I, as a femme-nâpew, survive the self that has normalized obliteration? Where is the "I" in the atomic nucleus of my warring ethics?

As an overweight child, I used to confess to manito that I wished they had made me a woman so I could jingle with haughtiness—self-determination becoming haute couture through the image of many of my aunties, who have been wonderfully rotund. I have waged combat with myself over why I call myself Two-Spirit instead of gay or queer; and I have had conversations with myself about what it means to paint myself ceremonially as femme. I do not call myself Two-Spirit to signify a romantic idealization of queer Indigeneity; I do it because I, and by extension this name I call myself, come from the red silk of the Red River. I do not perform femininity in order to quantify my queerness; I do it because there are days when I feel more feminine than masculine, and my femme-ness has always been more aggressive within me—and a tool I have often relied upon when navigating the corridors of institutions. I love my body, by which I mean my selves. I need to tell you that. It goes without saying that loving one's own Indigeneity is always a political act. And I write about my body in order to celebrate it, because all art is voyeurism. But still my body in its femme-ness often betrays me, and when I leave the gallery I am forced to ponder the ethics of such an owing and owning.

Which brings me back to artistry—for here, after all, I have been saying that my body is a tapestry. Maybe I cling to ekphrasis to make an emphasis: I own a body worth owing.

And perhaps I cling to art that is raked by destruction, reveals the surreal in real—which isn't so surreal after all, when we are faced with the earth dying and our futures maimed. I find excellence in interiority because my body is a marshland. And I find innovation in inward diving: Just what in hell is worth living for, in the moulding of bodies that are continually dying?

A Geography
of Queer Woundings

WHEN I FIND MYSELF in bouts of depression inked with anxiety, I lull my mind into an easy silence with music. "This is
what it looks like right before you fall," hums Mac Miller. "I
don't have no name, who am I to blame?" Miller's lyrics, which
come from his posthumous song "Circles," situate me in my
current predicament, here, during my own fall, which is a less
biblical one, more Indigenous. The last six months of 2019 were
a whirlwind of depressive bouts sprouting from loss, mourning,
sexual assault, abandonment, colonial violence, imperialism,
state-sanctioned genocide—all of which, for me, normalizes an
absurd fact of Indigenous life: it hurts to live. Trying to find joy,

I seek out others. I log in to Tinder, Grindr, Hinge, and Bumble. I go on dates, have casual encounters with others. And, in July 2019, I am forced to perform fellatio in the front seat of a car.

He and I are parked in the industrial area of Calgary. He is coming down from the high of Calgary Stampede machismo, all bravado and buckskin and PBR. We talked briefly on Grindr, me in a pocket of isolation, one where I've drained myself of confidence. I am doused in Viktor & Rolf cologne, a musky spice, making myself fungible and edible: two primary components of queer hookup culture. Devour me, I say, unlatch the maw and swallow me. I pang to be caressed, even in, or perhaps I mean to say amongst, the masochistic violence of anonymity and starved intimacy.

Beneath my grandmother, who looms above us with a dusty eye, the rumble of a CPR train drones by, and the hum of electrical boxes and generators fills the air—the soundscape of the city pollutes my cochlea, and Calgary betrays me, drowning out my whimpering "no" as the darkness of industry emerges, imperial. Here, the night cloaks whiteness, and I am granted my own death wish. In this moment, I think of the tattoo on Miller's left forearm that reads, "Only so much time left in this crazy world." I defeat myself and let him wrap himself up into me with a mallet culled of ermine to quicken his release—there is no softness here. I tell myself: *this is it, I've become a number.* Statistically, I become arithmetic here, removed from my body entirely. I float aromatically, watching myself, too, churn into industry, mechanical almost. I let him spill into my mouth and spit out a river of semen that quickly dries into a wash on the kokom scarf that's been torn from my head.

When I remove myself from the situation and return home, I crumble onto my carpet and cry into my dirtied scarf; I become arroyo, flash flood. *I thought I was going to die,* I repeat, and laugh maniacally until I terrify myself. This is what it looks like before I fall, crashing into matte fibre like a thunderstorm; I birth anew in a carpeted condominium, falling like Sky Woman did, except no one catches me here. I melt into the floorboards and am greeted by water bear. When they ask me my name, I reply, "I don't know"; that too has been stolen from me. "Just hold me awhile, won't you?" I ask of no one visible. And I am held epidermically by germs; this is all I can muster here where I have fallen, in this moss.

It's funny, I still talk to *you*—without your knowledge, of course—to ask with a pained valence: Why?

TO RELIEVE MY BODY of its disposability, I now find I am having to distance myself from queer life. I find no pleasure in hookup culture, I shy away from gay bars, I turn my eyes away from men who attempt to meet mine, I self-sabotage attempts anyone makes to get to know me intimately. I continually find myself asking: Am I queer enough to be queer? I try to deploy my gender, sexuality, and sex as ceremonious states of being—something I was taught by my epistemologies—so as to be cradled like a spirit plate, an offering of small portions for ephemeral hungers. Whiteness and masculinity are the crooks of queer culture, categorizing bodies into essences: thin, toned, or fat—the latter often categorized further into racialized preferences against blackness and brownness. As an Indigenous person I must interpolate annihilation into the throes of queer desire. My teeth are whitened from charcoal; here, even my mineralized skin becomes the buck on which you sharpen your incisors.

If writing autobiography is akin to literary voyeurism in the form of extraction through confession, then so too is this essay a form of extraction, hemorrhaging of the body, of its senses, its being pinpointed and acupunctured—mapped from crown to sole for the sake of readability here in this flailing, failing English. méscihkwekawiw, s/he hemorrhages or loses all of her/his blood. In the root of this word is mêsci, exhaustively, until all is gone, and from there I propel nêhiyâwewin into chinook: warm these frigid bones and cold, stilled, thickened blood—mêsikawiw, it has all leaked out, mêsciwasow, it melts or boils away. In this heating and ridding, where English enflames trauma to its boiling point, saturated and pressurized, I run from your properness, English. I want to move like a mirage and ghost myself beyond this structuring as this is an arena wherein spirits are eaten: ᐊᐧᐋᒥᐅᐅ᠊.

ᓂᐢ ᑲᕆᐣᐳᑎᕒᐤ ᐁᐧᔭᐧᐧ ᒥᕒᐤ ᐸᐢᑲᑭᓂᑲᐧ ᐁᑲᐧ ᑎᐣᒋᐧᐁᐧᔭᐧᐧᐢᒥᐨᐦᐊ ᑫᐧᐯᐦᐅᔭᐦᐢᑕᐦ᙮ᒥᐢᑫᕒᐧ

(Mirage. I leap beyond their consuming pages and destroy their precious eye.)

σ⅁ am reminded of a conversation σ⅁ once had, where σ⅁ am interpolated as "other" through the notation, "Josh, σ⅁ recognize ∇·ᵚᴨᒉ⅄° (wêhcisiw/it is easier) for me to navigate queerness because σᒉᐪᒉ (nimiyosin/I am standardly good-looking, attractive)." Whether P⅁ (kiya/you) mean to say it or not, what this tells σ⅁ is that my aestheticism is merely a curiosity, that desire for σ⅁ is simply a query, and queerness has limited room for ◁σP (aniki/those) outside the descriptors of "standardization": cisness, masculinity, whiteness, thinness. Like when σ⅁ adorn Savage Rose beadwork, a touch of This Claw, a flash of Mad Aunty, a Thunder Voice hat adorned with baby breath and sage, and decide to go dancing with friends— here, beneath the scrutiny of queerness, σ⅁° (niyaw/my body's) boundaries are violated when you grab σ⅁ earrings, touch σ⅁ coat, fondle σ⅁ hat, pull σ⅁ arm as if σ⅁ were the artifact and P⅁ the surveyor. Here, σ⅁ am the head within the scaffold, a cabinet of queerer curiosities. Queerness beheads σ⅁ in these situations much to the point σ⅁ am bereaved and σ⅁° reels back to that moment of breakage. So much of queerness has already beheaded itself in pixels—now P⅁ place the onus on σ⅁ to do the same, σ⅁ refuse to be dismembered: digitally, literarily, or literally.

Have P⅁ ever ◁·<ᵚCᶜ (wapahtam/witnessed) a ᒉ<⁺ ᴛᒉᵚ∆ᴐ∆·ᒉ (cîpay ni`mihitowin/ghost dance) to Doja Cat?— the only death that is dealt is to the non-human, the spirit, who loses yet another life, and σ⅁ am running out of hands to splay.

Or, perhaps ᓂᔭ mean to ask: ᐊᐁᐧᓇ (awina/who) names an event apocalyptic, here in the Christian stylizations of the word, meaning cataclysmic, and ᐊᐁᐧᓇ must this apocalypse affect in order for it to be thought of as "canon"? How do we pluralize such an apocalypse? Apocalypses as ellipses? ᐊᐁᐧᓇ is omitted from such a saving of space, ᐊᐁᐧᓇ material is relegated to the immaterial? Here too, ᓂᔭ craft a theory of Indigiqueerness by rejecting queer and LGBT as signposts of ᓂᔭ ᓀᐦᐃᔭᐃᐧᐃᐧᐣ (nêhiyâwiwin/my identity, NDNness), instead relying on the sovereignty of "traditional" language, such as Two-Spirit, and terminology ᓀᔭᓈᐣ (nîyanân/we) craft for ᓀᔭᓈᐣ, "Indigiqueer." How does queer Indigeneity upset or upend queerness? ᐊᐁᐧᓇ defines queerness and under ᐊᐁᐧᓇ banner does it fly? ᐊᐁᐧᓇ lands is it pocked within? ᓂᔭ churn these words over in my mouth, taste that queered ᓀᐦᐃᔭᐁᐧᐃᐧᐣ (nêhiyâwewin/Cree language) on ᓂᑌᔨᓂᐩ (nitêyiniy/my tongue), and wonder if ᐁᐧᔭᐚᐤ (wîyawâw/they) are enough. Like ᐚᓀᔨᐦᑕᒥᓵᔮᐃᐧᐣ (waneyi-htamisâyâwin), the ᓀᐦᐃᔭᐤ (nêhiyâw) word for queer, as in strange, but it is also defined as uncanny, unsettling; or ᐊᐧᓀᔨᐦᑕᒧᐦᐃᐁᐧᐃᐧᐣ (waneyihtamohiwewin), the act of deranging, perplexing—ᓂᔭ find Indigiqueerness a hinterland. ᓂᔭ like the fluidity, but my life is not a primer in performance: ᓂᔭ am fluid as ᓂᐯᐩ (nipîy/water), ᓂᐯᐩ ᐊᐁᐧᓇ owns itself, ᒥᔭᐤ (miyaw/body) ᐊᐁᐧᓇ owns itself, ᓂᔭ ᐊᐁᐧᓇ own myself. What does it mean to be Two-Spirit during apocalypse? What does it mean to search out romance at a pipeline protest—can ᓀᔭᓈᐣ have intimacy during doomsday? How do ᓀᔭᓈᐣ fuck in a sleeping bag outside city hall when the very ground is shaking beneath ᑐᕀᐋᐧ—military tanks and thunderous gallops, don't ᑭᕀ feel that resurgence contracting when ᑭᕀ inside? Perhaps, here too, ᓂᕀ play with apocalypse, eschewing eschaton, revelatory flirtations, uncovering its etymological webbings for ᓂᕀ am primed in this form of survival and resiliency work, having survived the end of the world(s) time and time again— this is but a blip in the codex of ᓂᕀ ancestral warrings and apocalypse is yet a tick upon this ᒥᔭᐤ (miyaw/body) ᓂᕀ call host. Here again ᓂᕀ become a phantom in this historical amnesia— ᓂᕀ will ᓂᐦᒁᑲᐣ (nihkwâkan, my face) to quartz and hope ᓂᕀ become the "crisis" of resistance, the tearing inherent within its etymological rooting: recovery or death. Sometimes ᓂᕀ find ᑭᕀ in the dreamscapes. Here too ᓂᕀ talk, whisper into ᑭᕀ ᒥᐦᑕᐊᐧᑲᕀ (mihtawakay/ear), "Never sleep again," in the hopes ᑭᕀ find ᓂᕀ a bladed glove, a clawed feral, when ᑭᕀ next contract ᑭᕀ seminal vesicles ᓂᕀ will you stones and sieve.

Sometimes ᓂᕀ the reddest in the shadows cast by ᓂᕀ ᒥᐦᒁᔭᐱ (mihkwayapi/blood vein).

ᓂᕀ in new york city, downtown Manhattan, in the Little Sister Hotel with a crush ᓂᕀ brought. Here, in this web of relations ᑐᕀᐋᐧ later let blow into the wind, ᑐᕀᐋᐧ practise an ethics of touching as a shared intimacy. In thinking about queerness, ᓂᕀ tire of resigning ᓂᕀ into preordained roles— top or bottom, dom or sub, masculine or feminine—and instead choose to see another whose sexual histories are aligned with

mine. ᓂᗭ wonder: When two bottoms fuck, do we angle ᑐᗴᐧᐤ
bodies towards a vector of queerness, queerness in its verb form,
active and animate, that intersplices ᑐᗴᐧᐤ into both a queer
past and future? But then again, my history as Indigiqueer has
limited scope here on Turtle Island—ᓂᗭ ᐊᐧᐃᐧᑲᐣᑲᐦ (wawi-
kankah/vertebrae) arc back towards creation. But it feels truly
radical to explore ᑐᗴᐧᐤ bodies outside the register of simple penetration, to consent to being cupped between ᒥᐸᐧᒻ
(mipwâm/the thigh), to taste the salt road of ᒥᑎᓯᐩ (mitisiy/
navel), to put pressure on perineum and bloom into thyme—all
womb and nerve endings.

   ᑐᗴᐧᐤ lie on ᑐᗴᐧᐤ ᒪᑌᐩ (nîyanân/our, matay/stomachs)
atop the bed facing one another. ᐯᗴᐊᐧᐤ pull up a *New York
Times* article: "The 36 Questions That Lead to Love." The night
prior, we are on Christopher Street dancing in Pieces to a
remixed version of Justin Bieber's "Yummy." A looping video
of ripped, naked white men plays in the background and everyone's eyes glance towards it every time they need a refill of
desire. A drag queen comes up to ᑐᗴᐧᐤ, ᑐᗴᐧᐤ are holding
ᓂᗭ and dancing, and asks, "So how long have you two fags
been together?" ᓂᗭ clear my throat, the word "fag" being one
ᓂᗭ don't like pinned onto ᓇᓴᑲᐩ (nasakay/my skin), but ᐯᗴᐊᐧᐤ
answer, with a stoic confidence, "Two months." It's the first time
ᑐᗴᐧᐤ attempted an answer, and ᓂᗭ resign ᓂᗭ to saying, "Yes,
okay, ᓂᗭ suppose ᑐᗴᐧᐤ "together." ᑭᗭ wrap yourself around
ᓂᗭ for the remainder of the evening, ᑐᗴᐧᐤ dance until even
ᑐᗴᐧᐤ pores cry in beheld joy. While ᑐᗴᐧᐤ on the bed, the

question "Name three things you and your ᓄᒋᒧᐢ (nîcimos/partner) appear to have in common" emerges from the article. ᓂᔭ ask ᑭᔭ how ᑭᔭ feel about that word, ᓄᒋᒧᐢ, ᑭᔭ tell ᓂᔭ ᑭᔭ prefer the word "interlocutor." ᓂᔭ resign myself back to a state of circumlocution, ᓄᔭᓈᐣ talk around the subject, and ᓂᔭ am never objective. Another question prompts ᑭᔭ to ask, "If a crystal ball could tell ᑭᔭ the truth about ᑭᔭ, your life, the future, or anything else, what would ᑭᔭ want to know?" But ᓂᔭ futurity is bound by finality; ᓂᔭ try to conjure affects of joy, companionship, success, but ᒥᔭᐤ betrays ᓂᔭ, and ᓂᔭ simply mutter, "Will ᓂᔭ ᐱᒪᑎᓯ (pimatisi/live?)" ᑭᔭ question ᓂᔭ, as ᓂᔭ have mumbled this answer, and ᓂᔭ raise ᓂᐢᑫᓯᐠ (niskîsik/my eye) to look at ᑭᔭ, blankly state, "ᓂᔭ ᐱᑯ ᐱᒪᑎᓯ"[1] (niya poko pimatisi).

ᓂᔭ have stolen the excitement from this unveiling act and neither of ᓄᔭᓈᐣ questions the immediacy of "have."

ᓄᔭᓈᐣ decide to go back to Christopher and drag-queen bingo at Stonewall. ᑭᔭ have never been here before, and ᓂᔭ am happy to lead ᑭᔭ into a site of queer history, rich with blackness, brownness, trans and non-binary excellence. ᓂᔭ revel in the affirmation ᑭᔭ receive as a non-binary person in this site that bubbles with trials and triumphs. ᓄᔭᓈᐣ go in, ᑭᔭ order ᓄᔭᓈᐣ a round of Stonewall Lager, and ᓄᔭᓈᐣ sit in the back. The hosting drag queen, an older queen and self-proclaimed insult comic, asks ᓄᔭᓈᐣ to come up to ᐏᔭ (wiya/s/he). ᐏᔭ asks how old ᐍᔭᐚᐤ are, if ᐍᔭᐚᐤ are together, and ultimately where

1 Aisha Sasha John's *I Have to Live* (McClelland & Stewart, 2017).

ᐍᔭᐚᐤ are from. ᐍᔭᐚᐤ note Canada and ᐏᔭ quickly looks to ᓂᔭ, here wearing my shirt that proclaims "ᓀᐦᐃᔭᐏᐏᐣ" and ᐏᔭ delves into the tired old jokes: "Do you live in tipis, what about igloos?" and ultimately, "So are you an Eskimo?" ᓂᔭ ᑎᐦᑎᐱᐸᔩᐤ ᓂᐢᑫᓯᐠ (tihtipipayiw niskîsik/I roll my eyes) and return to the table. ᓂᔭ begin to play the cards that are placed in front of ᓀᔭᓈᐣ, desperately trying to Indigenize the limited space around ᓂᔭ, call ᓂᔭ back into those bingo halls, call upon the slumbering bones of Manahatta and any Lenape within earshot. ᐍᔭᐚᐤ don't play ᐍᔭᐚᐤ cards, instead ᑭᔭ give them to ᓂᔭ, and ᑭᔭ watch an old Katharine Hepburn film while white twinks come up to ask if ᓀᔭᓈᐣ really Canadian—ᑭᔭ entertain them while ᓂᔭ withdraw to ᓂᔭ ᒥᐦᑕᐘᑲᐩ ᒥᐢᑎᑿᐢᑭᕽ (mihtawakay mistikwaskihk/eardrum) and wait for the beat of another B to be called.

IN CALGARY THIS WINTER, ᓂᔭ have decided to explore my sexuality on ᓂᔭ own terms, so ᓂᔭ am looking for sex toys down at a local sex shop and hair salon. The owner is doing a ᐃᐢᑵᐤ (iskwew/woman's) hair and smiles up at ᓂᔭ. ᓂᔭ nod back, that kind of nod that every prairie person understands as a greeting but only in passing so as to be left alone. ᓂᔭ in the back of the store, browsing dildos, a ᑲᐱᒫᐯᑲᐢᑌᓯᒥᐦᐟ ᐊᐍᔭᐠ (ka pimâpekastesimiht awîyak/prostate) massager, Fleshlights, wigs, whips, and handcuffs. Someone comes back to help ᓂᔭ, and ᓂᔭ ask where ᓂᔭ can find a ᒥᑕᑲᐩ (mitakay/penis) ring—ᓂᔭ feel the sexiest when ᓂᔭ linked to my own membership. The person helps ᓂᔭ

find a rubber ring, one without the cap on the bottom so it won't snap open when ᓂᔭ bind myself. ᓂᔭ begin to browse the rest of the shop; ᓂᔭ am feeling risky and empowered in ᓂᔭ curiosities. It's then ᓂᔭ hear two ᓈᐯᐤ (nâpewak/men) talking in the hair parlour of the shop about an upcoming date. "ᓂᔭ was asked out by an Aboriginal man, but I've never dated one of them before, have you?" His companion responds, "I haven't, but I mean, I'd try it?" and shrugs. The companion then looks over at me. "Hey you, over there." He raises his voice and points at ᓂᔭ. "What about you? Would you date an Aboriginal?" ᓂᔭ place the items back onto the shelf and move towards ᐍᔭᐚᐤ. "Well, ᓂᔭ am ᓀᐦᐃᔭᐃᐧᐃᐧᐣ so of course." To which everyone in the room stops talking and looks at ᓂᔭ, here ᓂᔭ am stripped and laid bare, naked as the histories written on ᓇᓴᑲᐩ (nasakay/my skin). "Oh, what kind?" "ᓂᔭᓀᐦᐃᔭᐃᐧᐃᐧᐣ," ᓂᔭ respond, ᓂᒋᐦᒋᐩ (nicihciy/my hands) beginning to shake, "from ᐅᐢᑌᓯᒫᐘᓯᓇᐦᐃᑲᐣ ᐯᔭᐠ" (ostêsimâwasinahikan peyak/Treaty 1). ᓂᔭ begin to make my way towards the door, until one hails me. "Wait, you're like perfect—are you single?" he asks. ᓂᔭ stop, momentarily, ᓂᐢᐱᐢᑿᐣ (nispiskwan/my back) to him, the sunlight pulling ᓂᔭ along by the little ᓀᐢᑕᑲᔭ (nêstakaya/hair) on ᓂᐢᐱᑐᐣ (nispiton/my arm). "Not for you," ᓂᔭ reply, and exit. What is witnessed in the room ᓂᔭ leave behind is a glob of ectoplasm exteriorized as ᓂᔭ leave ᓂᔭᐤ (niyaw/my body) and flee into ᑭᐢᑭᓯᐃᐧᐣ (kiskisiwin/memory); what is left in the room is a ᒥᑐᑲᐣ bone (mitokan miskan/pelvic bone) licked clean of tendon and three men playing Columbus to ᓂᔭᐘᓂᐦᒋᑫᐃᐧᐣ (wanihchikewin/my losses).

These days ᓂᐯ pickup line has been a Barthesian pun: to speak of love is to confront the muck of language.

IT'S JANUARY 2020 and ᓂᐯ am in Pennsylvania. ᓂᐯ invited to an event—"Solidarity Not Appropriation: Full-Metal Indigiqueer"—with a fellow Nádleehí Diné, for a conference hosted by UPenn's LGBT Center for the Martin Luther King Jr. Symposium on Social Change. There are many wonderful QTBIPOC folx in the Center and ᓂᐯ feel welcome for once in such a space designated as queer. ᓂᐯ filled with joy in being in ∇·ᐯᐺ·ᐤ Diné presence. ᓂᐯ conducting a reading and Q & A at the Kelly Writers House where, after ᓂᐯ reading, someone comes up to thank ᓂᐯ. "You're so inspiring," they note. "You know, I used to study the berdache"—using that outdated terminology of offence towards Two-Spirit/queer Indigenous histories. ᓂᐣᑎᐸᐧᐤ (nistikwân/my mind) immediately flows back to George Catlin's 1830 painting *Dance to the Berdache,* in which he announced that *this*—that is, queerness or Two-Spiritedness—is "one of the most unaccountable and disgusting customs that I have ever met in the Indian country . . . where I should wish that it might be extinguished before it be more fully recorded." Here the ceremonial flame ᓂᐯ carried from Mohkinstsis is so quickly extinguished, and ᓂᐯ a limp wick ready to be licked into yet another forceful slumber—Riel won't ᓂᐯ ᑯᐣᑯᐸᐧᔪᐃᐧᐤ (koskopawyowin/wake me) when ᑐᐯᑲᐤ are willing? Afterwards, ᓂᐯ find my Diné ᓂᐪᑌᒼ (nitôtem/friend). It is sublime how queer NDNs latch on to one another like magnets, that when ᐍᔭᐚᐤ find one another, ᐍᔭᐚᐤ run up against each other in such a way as to make ᐍᔮᐤ ᐯᔭᑰᐢᑳᐣ ᐹᐏᐦᑯᑖᑲᐣ (wîyâw peyakôskân pâwihkotâkan/their bodies a kind of kindling).

Afterwards, ᓂᔭ Diné ᓂᑑᑌᑦ and ᓂᔭ are both in the Penn Law House, which is this beautiful, ornate semi-Gothic historical building, for a panel on social change. This is single-handedly the most expansive and expensive building ᓂᔭ have ever set foot in—all marble, gold, and aged oak. Here the organizers asked, "So, how has your time at UPenn been?" and while ᓂᔭ am aware of the optics of gratitude, the emboldened statue of Columbus in full display down the street haunts ᓂᔭ, as if the statue is living, monumental and horrific, as if ᐏᔭ ears were ablaze from ᐏᔭ beckoning name and ᐏᔭ cold white head was peeking at us through the large stained glass windows. ᓂᔭ am empowered in the vicinity of kin; ᓂᔭ answer, "ᓂᔭ was just in that backroom sneaking out to have a cigarette because my anxiety was boiling. And it was boiling because ᓂᔭ am in a space that ᓂᔭ was never meant to be in, in an institution with an Indigenous academic population of less than 1 percent, with no classes regarding settler colonialism being offered, and in a place that trains lawyers to incarcerate black and brown peoples without the pedagogy or ethics to think through systemic and historical preconditioned ideologies. ᓂᔭ should not be here, and yet here ᓂᔭ am, sitting as the brief bridge to knowledge that ᐍᔭᐚᐤ all pining over—and for what? Will ᑭᔭ use it? Does my personal trauma of being the son of a father in and out of incarceration systems his whole life challenge you?"

Sometimes ceremony is two spirits ᒥᒥᐣᑫᐃᐧᐣ ᓂᓵᐦᑯᓂᐢᐠ (miciminkewin nîsôhkonisk/the act of holding hands) and never letting go in the pressurized state of empire's forearm. Sometimes ceremony is a lone drive on the highway and Buffy Sainte-Marie telling ᓂᐯ that god has always been a foot that can crush, and that magic never dies. Sometimes ceremony entails driving past Gimli, Manitoba, and the old graffiti sign that used to read "Honk if ᑭᐯ are horny" but now reads "Honk if ᑭᐯ are happy" and ᑭᐯ honk either way.

ᓂᐯ have taken non-Indigenous kin to see Tanya Tagaq. Many of these folks have told me afterwards that they felt terrified, as if they had just witnessed an exorcism. ᓂᐯ want to say: "ᑭᐯ have, of whiteness." Like New York City, this is now a test ᓂᐯ deploy more locally. Upon doing this, ᓂᐯ tell ᐁᐯᐸᐧᐤ, "If ᑭᐯ survive this, know ᐅᐯᐦᐤ will not." Driving home, ᓂᐯ find myself unable to summon a word. One of ᑭᐯ will ask, "What's wrong?" ᓂᐯ will try to talk, but ᓂᐯ ᒥᑐᐧ (mouth) will open galactic, like a well ᑭᐯ continually pour ᑭᐯ into ᓂᐯ, talking louder, more intensely, in longer bursts with sharpened punctuation. ᓂᐯ strangle from grammatology. ᓂᐯ am betrothed to linguistic entanglements to the point that verbs begin to mutate beneath ᓂᐟᐁᔨᓂᐩ (nitêyiniy/my tongue). ᓂᐯ find myself saying ᓂᐯ "woundered" instead of "wondered." How does one caretake for ᐯᑭᐢᒁᐃᐧᓂᐢ (pîkiskwewinis/a word), or ᐊᐢᑮ (askiy/world), when ᒥᑎᐩ

(mitisiy/the navel) is such an ᐊᕑᐃᐧᐃᐧᔭ ᒥᒍᔭ (nayawiwin mitôn/exhausted mouth)?

A memory emerges here to instruct: ᓂᕁ am trying to make bannock the way the women in my family do—hands a mimicry of femininity. Slightly burned around the edges and bottom, ᓂᕁ feed ᑭᕁ, ᑭᕁ tell ᓂᕁ ᑭᕁ like it, but ᓂᕁ know it's soured from too much lard. ᓂᕁ say, "This is no good," and want to immediately burst into tears, yet ᑭᕁ continually reassure me it's delicious. ᓂᕁ say, "You don't understand. I've gambled my bodies just to make this." ᑭᕁ don't question the weight of "this" because it's a gravity foreign to ᑭᕁ own. Then when ᓂᕁ come back, ᓂᕁ finally know how to answer. "Have ᑭᕁ ever wondered why ᑭᕁ see bones when ᑭᕁ turn ᓂᕁ on?" ᓂᕁ will ask, "Where dirty talk becomes an obsequy?" ᓂᕁ want to ask if ᑭᕁ have ever opened ᑭᕁ eyes when ᑭᕁ are beside ᓂᕁ to see that ᓂᕁ am sometimes a skull in a flower bed—blown righteous with holes?

"What's wrong," ᓂᕁ will reply, "is that ᑭᕁ speak so much, ᑭᕁ drown ᓂᕁ."

"What's wrong," ᓂᕁ will reiterate, "is that ᑭᕁ have never died—least of all in ᓂᐢᑎᑭᐗᐣ (nistikiwân/my mind)."

The Year in
Video Gaming

IN 2016, MY maternal family lost a great matriarch, who died
after years of living as a paraplegic. After the loss, my mother
and father permanently took in two of my aunt's children, now
my cousin-siblings, both of whom had lived with us, although
"temporarily," since they were children. I have such fervour for
those two, who came from trauma and survived against all odds
as a baby and a toddler. They are now teenagers, but I see the
ways in which their mental health has suffered: one has social
phobias, and the other anxiety and panic attacks. Both have
clung to video games as a medium for escapism, entertainment,
and social enrichment. Their medium of choice? *Fortnite*.

Developed by Epic Games in 2017, *Fortnite* is a massive, multi-player shooter-survival video game in which upwards of a hundred players, yourself included, are enmeshed in a hyper-comic world wherein a battle royal ensues until only you remain (whether alone, or in a duo, or as a squad of up to four players). *Fortnite* has been ranked one of the most popular games of all time, with an estimated 250 million online registered players. Both my cousin-kin, and many other folks in my life, have attached themselves to this game, playing with friends near and far into the wee hours of the night to win that battle royale. How I watched them cheer, laugh, scream in anger, and create strong social bonds regionally and globally with players they've grown attached to, talked to online, and made community with.

Then, in its tenth season, on October 13, 2019, *Fortnite* got sucked suddenly into a black hole, its web of relations stolen (albeit temporarily, as we now know) without recompense or notification. This, of course, was a marketing ploy by Epic Games in order to usher in their new season. *Fortnite* stayed offline for two days, but for many it was as if the end had come, without rhyme or reason. For my cousin-kin, it was apocalyptic. I witnessed how their mental health issues crept back up to them, as their most relied-upon tool for finding stability had been stolen from beneath their very analogues. I wondered: Could such a disappearing act be felt as violence? It surely seemed that way. My kin mourned, their lovely second life swept up into a rapture, pixels embodying people in a digital cleansing.

I speak of this only as a preface to observing our—and even more so the younger generations'—reliance upon escapism while in the throes of fantasy. Ever since the inclusion of "gaming disorder" in the eleventh revision of the World Health Organization's International Classification of Diseases, I pay attention to the ways in which video games have become coping mechanisms for bubbling or buried valences of mental health, primarily anxiety and depression. These are mechanisms I too have used and continue to use throughout my life in order to escape being housed within a body—a physical one, but also a cultural, racialized, sexualized, and Indigenized one—that the world often likes to disengage from. As a youth I would flock to the local library for access to the Internet, where I would engage in online arenas of gaming and socializing through such websites as Pogo.com and Neopets. Keenly, I'd check back every day or two to continue with and stay alongside the communities I had built in these pockets of pixels.

As a teenager, I incessantly played the MMORPG *Lineage II*, a fantastical role-playing game wherein you made an avatar—mine was an Orc named Zoa (the progenitor of the protagonist of my book *full-metal indigiqueer*)—and fostered a beautiful ring of kinship. Mine was with folks I played with across North America, creating a "clan" system. Together we would hunt for treasure, level up (a.k.a. "grind"), go on large-scale raids, and often lounge around in the digital pastures of the game's idylls, taking pictures, talking about our personal lives, and sharing stories. This, to me, was a sovereign way of owning a body I had been taught to distrust because I was queer, Indigenous, and fat. I re-created myself as an imagined embodiment of pixels: here I was a muscle queen, a femme Orc with a red mohawk, a monk (often a "brawler" class) who wielded round, sharpened chakrams in both of her fists. I was powerful, haughty, righteous in my beings—though I never really learned to take that much further than the computer screen, at least until adulthood. All this came to an abrupt halt when I was no longer able to afford the monthly fee to play the game and thus had to foreclose my account indefinitely—and what followed was a tremendous period of mourning, as I had lost the kinships I fostered in those worlds.

I still think there are healthy benefits to gaming. In moderation, one can learn how to become socially and healthily adept in the worlds we inhabit beyond the realms of coding, and to find solace to deal with and unpack mental health traumas. In the summer of 2019, I relied heavily upon video games in order to rejuvenate and heal the central tenets of my being through, perhaps, a type of stasis. In my experience, gaming is much like charging one's self: the body becomes a console, plugged into its outlet, and it recharges while the mind is removed from the whirlwinds of its mental imaginings—the webbing cracks in its exoskeleton that have formed after the shower of rocks thrown at us in our daily lives—and placed instead into the realm of its wildest imagination. It's funny how the mind can be transplanted into, and live vicariously through, a body foreign to its own, how we can inhabit a Strife[1], a Redfield[2], or a Croft[3], and exist simultaneously within two worlds—a lesson I am also learning through my own nêhiyâw ways of being within multiple oralities, temporalities, and continuums in a single moment.

I spent much of my summer playing *Fire Emblem: Three Houses*, made by Koei Tecmo and released on July 26 of that year. The *Fire Emblem* series is a highly popular JRPG (Japanese role-playing game) wherein you take control of an often amnesiac protagonist, who is the saviour of the world. You are plunged into a space rife with political strife and warfare. In *Three Houses*, you can play as either a female or a male protagonist named Byleth (though you are free to rename them) within the continent of Fódlan, which is divided into three rival nations at peace after a period of warfare brought about by the archbishop of the Garreg Mach Monastery, a central hub between all three nations. You begin as a mercenary in training under your father, Jeralt, an infamous ex-knight of the Monastery, and are quickly hired as a professor within the Monastery—which is also an academy full of students from

---

[1] *Final Fantasy VII*'s Cloud Strife (a remastered version to be released in 2020 but shown at E3 in 2019)

[2] *Resident Evil*'s Redfield siblings: Claire and Chris (remastered and released in 2019)

[3] The popular female protagonist Lara Croft, most notable in her recent release in 2018

all three nations. You begin the game by picking a nation to ally with, and become the head teacher of their class, though you are able to enrol students whom you impress from other nations as you progress. The important thing in this game, though, is its support system, wherein you form friendships and rivalries with your students. This is key: you unlock their backstories and connect on an emotional and personal level with their development. Midway through the game, a time-skip happens, and your character is plunged into stasis while your students age into adulthood.

After the time-skip, you re-emerge and find your students again, only to partake in the now global warfare that is taking place between all three nations and a fallen Monastery. Here you can side with your nation or with the Monastery to help rebuild (though I often chose to forgo the religiosity of the Monastery in order to practise a campy form of digital decolonization). Now, because you are no longer a teacher but a colleague of your previous students, your mutual support eventually allows you to woo, romance, and marry them. The game features an allowance for queer romance within its storylines, a single one for male players and several for female players.

I played as the male Byleth (whom I renamed Zoa) and enjoyed the narrative of the game, but in my despondence and my rupturing of some of my relationships, I felt it most important to use the game as a medicinal tool. I spent countless hours first teaching, gift-giving, and chatting with the only male-romance option, Linhardt, a genius researcher and scholar who flutters between academic interests and is privy to exhaustion, to the point that he will doze off if you bore him—all the while adamantly scheduling nap times (a very astute grad school tactic, if you ask me). He constantly ponders the ethics and moral decisions around his research (a decolonialist again, if you ask me), and that research's applications within and beyond the ivory tower of his academia. Much of my free time was spent logging on to the game to see Linhardt, and to talk about reading, fishing, sweets, sleep, and research.

Post time-skip, Linhardt is twenty-one, and my character is of a similar age. I spent my time wooing him in a Fódlan now ruined by civil war and religiosity. We chatted on the battlefield and in refuges about the state of affairs in the world, and about academia's role in global warfare. Linhardt is a romantic, and after the war is won, he will propose to you if you have a high enough support role—which I did. On September 8, 2019, I posted to my Instagram that after seventy hours I had found a digital nîcimos (lover/partner) who had asked, "Would you spend [your] time with me? I want to know more about you, I want to solve the mysteries that surround you, I don't think I'll ever meet anyone more intoxicating than yourself." While filming this touching scene, I was awed. After accepting his proposal, I was given a still of Linhardt lying in the grass, gazing at me, noting, "It may be some time until we can nap beneath a tree, peaceful sunlight filtering through the branches, but when that day comes, to have you there lying by my side? Paradise. And we will have made it so."

While the politics, mechanics, and animations of the game may sound mundane—in a sense, they are—as I noted earlier, I found healthy and bountiful benefits in the realm of video gaming, benefits that are very real. The game is a fundamental practice of self-reflection, queer desire, embodiment (digital and physical), and mental health. I say this because it allowed my body to rest while I played, refocusing the energies of my whirling mind—one racked with anxiety, depression, mourning, and loss—and to channel its energies into something constructive and enriching: into narrative, plot, metaphor, and agency; and because the game also asked me to self-reflect on my own desires. What is it I want and need from the world, as a Two-Spirit Oji-nêhiyaw nâpew?

I am overtly romantic, but as a writer, academic, editor, grad student, and one who often travels for community engagement, it is a pipe dream to think of having the luxury to spend an afternoon, much less an entire day, lounging around and napping beneath a tree with any future nîcimos. That said, the idea of stasis, a moment of cathartic encapsulation within the spaces of our relations—that is, the biosphere, askiy, mistik, or what you may call the "idyll"—seems wholeheartedly akin to how we would think about relationalities through nêhiyâwewin. That is, to love, sâkihitin, is a summoning of being, perhaps one of braids, into the world that we animate and are accountable to; it becomes more than simply a Western act of speaking. It is a sacred animation. And such a summoning into orality within the spaces of askiy could be considered an act of wahkohtowin—or enacting relationality within a world, here meaning the land, that asks for us all to humble ourselves, moving away from the hierarchy of being wherein "human" is crowned atop a vertical ladder, and instead link hand in hand as a rhizome, a plurality of linkages that come together horizontally as "all my relations." And this, done together through sâkihitin and wahkohtowin, would be what I consider miyopimatisowin, or "the good life," an act of being in ethical, respectful, and reciprocal relations with all those we hold as animations (beyond what Western epistemologies would consider inanimate, such as trees, rivers, rocks, sky). The video game doesn't state this, but isn't that the beauty of literature or narrative? It's a type of virtual play on the page or on the screen, and we, as readers or gamers, plug into a world ripe with possibilities and seed our subjectivities into the carefully crafted vantage points that plot always leaves open for us.

Even as *Fire Emblem: Three Houses* taught me to question my own desires in terms of relations, it also mended my body, soothed my razing mind, and corrected my blurred perspectives into clearer optics, freer prairies. Perhaps, yes, fantasy and gaming are coping mechanisms, but what I've come to learn through this mechanism is that pimâtisowin, or the act of living, is about coming to and into an embodied world that acts much like a virtual one. We are always butting (and budding) up against the coping mechanisms of others: how they perform, their speech acts, how they respond to us, inquire about us, answer us, ignore us, treat us, respect us. Video games taught me to think ethically about engagement, how to converse properly with someone who houses traumas and has been taught, or self-taught, to act, reply, or respond in certain ways to particular cues—much as I had to select correct and respectful answers when wooing and romancing Linhardt. The game asked me very personal questions about how I want to navigate the world of queerness as an Indigenous person who is trying to root themselves into nêhiyaw epistemologies, to treat sex, gender, and sexuality as sacred beings, much like sâkihitin, so as not to become fungible, disposable, usable or co-opted into the maw of settler sexualities: i.e., so an not to become pixelated into appropriation on Grindr and its tribologies, not become fetishized as nobly savage, avoid becoming missing or murdered, and to forgo sexual violence.

Recently, on a trip home from Saskatoon's Ânskohk Indigenous Literature Festival, I revelled in the glory of #NDNJoy with Indigenous women and queers. Flying back to Calgary, I sat with my dear kin Billy-Ray Belcourt and we haughtily, unabashedly, and noisily discussed the politics and livelihoods of surviving and living as queer Indigenous nâpewak amongst an audience of mostly non-Indigenous men (one of whom, seated behind us, then leaned in to listen). We talked about sex, sexualities, partners, desire, and joy—it was marvellous, and truly one of the most medicinal conversations I've been privileged to have. We asked, and this is also what *Fire Emblem* asked of me: "Am I queer enough to be queer?" While my embodiment as Byleth/Zoa wooing the napping genius

Linhardt was part of me thinking about relationality, I was also pondering futurities and boundaries (both of which are bound up and hyperbolized by anxiety—which can be read as an incessant fear about, or distrust in, the existence of a visible future[4]). I wanted the monogamy, solitude, and static of a moment unencumbered by either past or future—a moment, beneath a tree, wholeheartedly embraced by the plethora of relations blossoming into being around us in a land sovereign to its own found families: a queer utopia, perhaps, if we think of the biosphere as a cavalcade of families made from native and invasive species living in relative harmony, and not only for a singular moment.

Linhardt and Byleth—and the simplicity of a nap turned into paradise, churned into continuums crafted by two in synchronized relation to one another and to their surrounding others. You may criticize this as homonormativity—which perhaps it is, seemingly striving towards heterosexual traditions— but then, I think that "queerness" is not a word we know in nêhiyâwewin. While surely we had polyamory, and what we would now consider queer couplings, we did so to continue the bounty of community and the reciprocal care that it took to remain within the tenets of miyopimatisowin. And I recognize the importance of having queer bars, of having ease of access to "hookup culture," of the sense of the fleetingness of living that emerged from the trauma of HIV/AIDS and the need to come

---

[4] From Anna Mehler Paperny's *Hello I Want to Die Please Fix Me: Depression in the First Person* (Penguin Random House Canada, 2019).

up with a sustainable way of relating, and of the shifting dynamics of found families. But I also want and need more than all that from this noun and verb, "queer." I envision myself, perhaps, as a queer kokom, one who maintains the rigidity of a family, queer or not, singular and communal, through the foundational framework of a relationship turned bedrock.

So, I return to Linhardt, to Billy-Ray, whether human or not, and ask again: Am I queer enough to be queer? Perhaps the answer is no. But also, perhaps the answer is yes. Yes, we are making strides, strategically planning our next moves, and emerging into the world(s) ripped from the hands of the Two-Spirited since 1492. Inasmuch as the future of Indigiqueerness is ours for the making, we define it on our own terms, sovereignly, singularly, and collectively. What I need to survive, most of all right now, is for queerness to mean something more than consumption and hierarchical striving. I need it to be like Byleth and Linhardt, a landscape ripe with conditions of possibilities for the future—however it may look or feel for my kin to root into being.

And in moving forward, all I can say is kiyâm—"let it be, it's okay, let's go, then"—which is also a root for "quietly." So it means to listen, to avoid making noise—quietness of being asking us to listen fiercely and to respond in whatever way the body so chooses, but also in a way that is endowed with respect and reciprocity. For me, this is kiyâm: the quietness of being in my living room, bear root tea in hand, the body healing, the mind solidified, and the spirit of me braided into the zeitgeist of virtuality. In the aftermath of a video game, by which I also mean this essay, I find myself ready to emerge afresh, anew, and aglow from a screen of pixels and a well-rested body crusted with mineral.

Writing as
a Rupture

I HAVE LONG ARGUED that the physical body we inhabit, in its zippered coat of skin, will always be tied to the body of text we create—and I think this particularly true for BIPOC (Black, Indigenous, and peoples of colour), disabled, queer, and/or women (and any intersection therein) writers. We don't have the ability to write simply of aesthetics. I can never write a poem about the shapeliness of a teacup for the sake of the teacup. For me, such cuppings are always bound by political poetics because of two truths: one, that settler colonialism and heteropatriarchy have failed; and two, that my existence has and will always be a radical act of political livelihood. So much so that, when I write, I write from the body, proprioception; story is attached to me integrally, umbilically, and we feed and nourish one another like regurgitant birds.

I also contend that to think one is a master—while running a "master" class, for example, or even desiring to "master" craft—is wholly violent.[1] Stories are oratory, even when written on the page, for they require animations in order to live—and such animations, in nêhiyaw fashion, make story an animate being, living vocabulary, kin we are accountable to. I refuse to trauma-bond with stories I hold like lovers. Dare I place a possessive "my" when acknowledging *my* stories? Such possession rouses in me a wick that feels like wildfire.

How, then, is storying akin to lovemaking?

Let's say you find me beautiful, but you are only able to comment on the aesthetic, not the animations, of my skin-story: what an emptied adjective: "beautiful." To say it with merit you'd need to know how the bodybook enfolds me, spines engorged and enveloped. You would need my body to challenge you, fatally so, to the point where it asks you to rethink that recycled verb, "love," and in lieu asks you about the weight of that noun, "loss." All while pondering, through the lens of a foggy camera or a misting iris: Where is the fascinating pornography of the world? And who is the flawed auteur?

Instead, let me make a universe of a freckle. Let me focus less on the grand and more on the mundane; entire bodies of

---

[1] See Audre Lorde's *The Master's Tools Will Never Dismantle the Master's House.*

rich stories are written in the minute. I respect in a writer, as much as I respect in a lover, the ways in which languages mix with odour—and therefore I am forever huffing oratory. I find storying is often a series of attractions. Like when I undress you and bear witness to your majesty. I don't feign a bow to monarchy—this particular "you" being European—but rather ask: "How does any single body exist so multifariously?" You reply coyly, as if this compliment strikes a tender tendon, and brush it off. I shy away, so as not to embarrass you. I turn off the lights and know in the tasting of a vowel on your nipple, the perfume of syntax wafting from the oils in your skin, that a body, in all its glories, wrecked and steadfast, is alit here in the dark with language, euphemism, allegory. I trace your body as I would a map, spelling homebound in a clavicle, and wayfinding boisterously because I am not ready for rest.

This, I think, is an entry point into poetics.

Which came first, though, the poetic or the erotic?

I am looking for "me," but I've hidden bits of myself in each of "you," that universal pronoun—and I unfold like a crane, intricately, delicately, into origami, originality.

READERS OF MY WORK have sometimes noted that they are unable to differentiate between the poetic, prosaic, theoretical, or autobiographical in my books. During my time with the annual book competition Canada Reads, which is broadcast on national radio, I was often mistaken for my novel's protagonist, Jonny, instead of being hailed as Joshua—a familiar quandary since the publication of my book *Jonny Appleseed*. Although it is clearly called "A Novel" on the cover, it is readily accessed by readers as autobiographical; whereas in my collection of poems *full-metal indigiqueer*, a text that is perhaps more personally aligned with the histories of my life, "my" voice is veiled behind the character of Zoa, its speaker, who never overlaps as a persona or identity-appendage of me as writer, speaker, thinker, or orator.

As for this new work of storying, the work of this book: Do I call it biographical? Autofiction? Autobiographical? I lean towards the categorization, if I must categorize at all within the landscapes of literary productions and academic pageantries, of "biostory." The work of academia and writing for an Indigenous and Two-Spirit person is that of continually ghosting one's self through barriers; it is the work of being held like a spider in a web of its own trappings, held tightly within a kaleidoscope of octagonal optics; it is the work of projecting a spider's vision onto its own productions, and from its own proteins spinning silk and kinship. I feel I must make my own literary fields, then theorize, publish, and defend them to committees or companies. Why does this seem so difficult? For surely others have easily slid through this semicolon—and yet, to me, it feels as if a life is on the line. The body, the text, the dissemination, the seminal labour, the community formation, the kinship extension.

Philippe Lejeune refers to autobiography as a "contractual genre depending upon distinct codes of transmission and reception." Autobiography as a form and genre becomes a declaration of absoluteness that firmly anchors the "I" of a narrative and binds it to the writer as truth-teller. Lejeune discusses the autobiographical pact as a suggestion that the "author's signature is a declaration of autographical intension . . . [is] a promise to the reader that the textual and the referential 'I' are one." But I take offence with this pact-making. I do not take lightly, as an Indigenous writer let alone an Indigenous person, the expectation to form a pact without consent, that my oratories be bound to a page, the page given spine and barcode, the marketing of biography met with the scalpels and magnifying glass of inspector and voyeur, and my body intertwined in the lacings of verso and recto. I ask: Is autobiography a treaty-making, if the treatise is the narrator as subject? Is the treatise of such a treaty the desire to petrify and archive? What forms of colonial violence do I underpin when I mark myself with form and genre as glyph and brand?

Joanne Saul, in *Writing the Roaming Subject*, argues that "genres are never innocent or naïve but rather are formal constructs implicated in the very processes of ideological production." What of genre and its historical productions, what of the *then* and *now* of language and of contract? Of treatise and of treaty? Etymologically, "genre" flints from the Latin *genus*, meaning birth, family, nation; Old French *gendre*, here translating into "son-in-law"; and the Proto-Indo-European *génhos*, meaning race, lineage, and sharing a doublet with "gender." Is genre, under institutional ideologies, a violent categorizing this way? To be the treatise of this nation-building, to signify genus as an Indigenous writer and thinker, is to surrender to a romanticization of Indigeneity—Indigeneity as flora and fauna. Perhaps genre is also a means of indoctrination for me: into apocalypse, revelation. To be categorized by racial lineages, to be cauterized within the hyphen of "Pan-Indigenous," is also to forgo the historical futurities of Indigenous concepts of gender and sexualities. I refuse to put my signature upon the ledger of genre; I refuse to be X or chromosome. I am Indigenous and gendered beyond Western understandings, beyond sex and nation and nuclear categorizations. And I find fault in the evolution of this form we call autobiography; I take offence at the impulse to identify my writings, and that of so many other BIPOC writers, by genre or as pulp. Our writings are more than lignin and fibre. To call genre naive or innocent, as many do, is nothing more than a quaint way of ignoring the colonial imperative behind literary and academic publishing—a colonial imperative that theorizes or aestheticizes this land we call Turtle Island. Do not categorize my stories within this cauterization, this boundary of genre and form. It is a means of division: genre as sovereign, maniac monarch. Making naive the Native here is a way of laying claim to the multiplicity of bodies within this noun we call text—discombobulated etchings on the treatise and the treaty.

If autobiography is a means of authorizing the treatise; if the powers of institutions through publication or recommendation can make an author into an authoritarian (as a contributor to the genus of this nation's historical archive); then in what ways is an autobiography also an obituary? In what ways is self-narration imbued with nationhood? In what ways is autobiography a means of legitimizing and solidifying the ideas and bodies of Indigenous peoples and lands into the preserving amber of literary national land claims? "Official multiculturalism," Saul notes, "insists that the subject stays still . . . [E]thnic subjectivity, understood and contained in collective terms, is always determined by reference to a distant, and often dehistoricized past." Saul is discussing the connection between the rise in biotexts through the works of Fred Wah, Roy Kiyooka, Daphne Marlatt, and Michael Ondaatje and these writers' disruption of the boundaries and borders of genre throughout their literary and political lives in the form of experimental poetics, the long poem, and biotextual writing that layers together travel narrative, letters, family history, cultural politics, high theory, poetics, and prose. I find myself in an impasse alongside all these writers, although in a different register, as I try to contextualize what a biotext might mean for me, and for Indigenous writing altogether. If autobiography is the poetics of belonging in a Canadian context, biotextual writing seeks to disobey and demarcate that belonging and subservience. In nêhiyâwewin we have no word for autobiography. We have the verb masinahike, to write; and masinahwew, s/he marks for him/her, which is akin to biography within contemporary understanding. Here too, our concepts of auto and biography are braided together through the act of writing and of marking:

a pictograph or a petroglyph are story, historical, and commu-
nally so, because the body of the storyteller is never removed
from the bodies of their landbase, riverbase, oceanbase. Knowing
this, I have never sought to call myself novelist, poet, essayist,
or academic. Rather, I have pinned myself to the concept of
an otâcimow, a storyteller, something that may sound simple in
English but in nêhiyâwewin denotes in its root, otâci, that we
are not only storiers but also legend-speakers. Which is to say
we are historians and cultural theorists, informers; which is
also to say we are academics and researchers and confessors;
which is also to say that we are journalists and poets. If autobiography within Western linguistic systems is an obituary,
then in nêhiyâwewin it is a wildly engendered genre of returning and of revival; of transplanting the past into the future and
glimmering in the hope of "now."

You can find me in the archives of silt and pickerel.

I CALL THE now-blossoming oeuvre of my creative writing
"sibling stories," wherein each story leads me to its relations.
While writing my first book, the volume of poetry *full-metal
indigiqueer*, my editor and I removed a handful of poems that
were animated sensually—I call them "the beach scenes."
These poems didn't quite fit with the tone and overall arc of
the book. But later I returned to those beach poems and used
them as the progenitor of the novel that followed, *Jonny
Appleseed*. In the writing of the novel, those little poems unfurled
into Jonny's childhood and queer blossoming. I also think of

Jonny as the human counterpart to the virtual character of Zoa, the protagonist and speaker in *full-metal*. The two books talk to one another, they cross over, they exist in the same literary universe, and I have let my stories lead me where they need to go. I think that's my role as an otâcimow—to listen fiercely to characters and simply animate them as they wish to be. And this is what has led me to this current book, inasmuch as the character of Jonny taught me a valuable lesson through their storyhood: "a humility is just a humiliation you loved so much it transformed." I have used this phrase as a guiding principle in my life. In thinking about how I relate to my mental well-being, I began asking myself: How can I be accountable to that which we consider damning? Or how can I be in a healthy and reciprocal relationship with that which we stigmatize? I would go so far as to call Jonny a character so embryonically tied to me as a person that he posits himself on the ledge between biography and fiction. As I wrote about his struggles with mental health—although in fictionalized and hyperbolized forms, some of which are not my own—he became an avatar for me, the writer, a way of making material, or at least helping verbalize, that which I so expertly hid within the linings of my own body. For example, I now ask: How does insomnia serve me, as a storyteller, if I can find healthy ways to engage with it? How do I navigate anxiety and its attendant waves of panic to think of it as an ancestral communicator? Or, perhaps, to think of it as a coping mechanism for survival? If we animate our "mental health" and think of its effects as kin rather than parasitic, can we make love to them, transform them?

I also find it essential to discuss concepts of mental health within Indigenous ways of being; and to think about the stigmatization of depression, anxiety, and all mental struggle in ways that are a gifting back to community, and primarily to Indigenous youth, who are committing suicide at alarming rates across Turtle Island. I come to this decision in part because of my own experiences working with youth. While living in Manitoba, I worked for the local Friendship Centre and ran the youth drop-in where we'd teach kids cooking, lead cultural activities, help them with their resumés, and, most importantly, provide them with a safe place to get together. There, one of our youth nearly overdosed on opioids while sitting at a desk. Thankfully, we were able to call an ambulance immediately and get him help. After healing, he returned to the centre and, when asked by us what happened, he shrugged, "I just thought that this was a natural part of growing up." After that, I constantly asked myself: What kind of pain does a young teenaged boy have to be in to be addicted to painkillers? Why is an inherent gamble with death normalized as a means of growing into Indigenous adulthood, particularly its masculinities? Is a youth still a "youth" if they have nearly killed themselves from a self-induced overdose? I hear Aila, a child character played by Kawennáhere Devery Jacobs in the film *Rhymes for Young Ghouls*, who announces, upon witnessing her mother's suicide, "That day, I aged by a thousand years." What means

"innocence" for Indigenous childhood development if our
youth age in a sped-up register of time that propels them
towards death? And just why did we have difficulty around
the topic of this youth's mental health? This memory has sat
with me ever since—and that is when the stories and mental
unhealth I house like kin, that I shy away from, that terrify me
to the point of isolation, come rushing forward into oratory.

I initially turned towards creative non-fiction to engage
with these topics in ways I feel are ethical, responsible, and
reciprocal—though, as I will explain, I have turned rogue
within this form and genre, and instead now wear the cloak
of nêhiyâwewin as an otâcimow. In my previous two books,
I often hid behind character to explore stories of personal
trauma that were hyperbolized for the sake of plot or glamorized for tone—but this is a kind of violent disservice to one's
own truths. Perhaps I came to this book out of necessity,
inasmuch as my mental health—a primary component to my
overall well-being, within the cyclical nêhiyaw medicinal-wheel
teachings of holistic health: spiritual, physical, emotional, and,
lastly, mental—has been so negatively impacted through the act
of writing, sharing, touring, and interrogation that I now find
myself with no other avenue to explore.

I recall, for example, being on tour in Toronto with *Jonny
Appleseed* and doing several interviews with local reporters.
As I have noted, Jonny is a character very much embroiled with
my own histories, my own experiences, to the point where
I am often mistaken for Jonny himself (several interviewers,

while asking me questions, have called me Jonny; and I have encountered this confusion in brief romantic encounters as well). One of the perplexing things that interests me in the contemporary consumption of BIPOC and queer writing is that our texts are readily misread as confession, non-fiction, memoir, boudoir.

While in Toronto, a reporter, having researched me thoroughly, asked: "So Josh, can you tell me how the death of your grandmother has influenced your novel?" Being a fledgling writer at the time, I accommodated the request and reluctantly retold the story of my grandmother's murder in the sixties—at which the reporter nodded, jotted down notes, quickly thanked me, and said goodbye. What has shaken me about this experience is that it was not the first time that type of extractive questioning about personal histories and my experiences with trauma has cropped up, nor will it be the last, and while the reporter maintained their agency and left unencumbered by wounds, all set with fresh insight into their critical angle about my book, I found myself in downtown Toronto racked with grief and holding myself through a particularly intense anxiety attack. It was a slaughtering. I felt disembodied, I reeled amongst an onslaught of noise pollution: honking cars, pedestrian babble, sirens, the heavy rumble of a train. I found myself in Toronto's downtown shopping mall, the Eaton Centre, sitting in the food court sobbing uncontrollably, much to the dismay of those eating fast food around me.

How can the inquisition for and distribution of knowledge be anything but a type of assault if not done with protocol and ethics? How are queer Indigenous writers, many of whom are at the forefront of a new generation in contemporary literature, made to be wholly disposable under the guise of benevolence and diversity? How does the purchase of a novel—such as my own, here in Canada selling for eighteen dollars—allow for a type of permission on the part of the consumer to have unbridled access to a writer's life, to survey our bodies as if we were objects of curiosity? How does this very manuscript I am writing now also position me upon the metaphorical medical table, primed for inspection and autopsy?

How does such disposability link or braid with our understandings of MMIWG2S[2]?

I must remember that a story can be eaten like a body.

Perhaps I mean to say that being a writer under the banner of "Literature" when you are a queer Indigenous person is to create a type of peeping, voyeurism, stripping, the expectation of the unveiling of bodies, histories, communities, traumas. Creative non-fiction fails me here, as did the novel, as did poetry, as do the larger boundaries and borders of genre and form—I stylize and characterize myself and my writings within the webbings of my ancestral and contemporary otâcimowak in an attempt to answer some of these questions, to unpack these expectations, to lay claim to the sovereignty my body houses,

---

[2] Missing and Murdered Indigenous Women, Girls, and Two-Spirited People

and, if I must strip, to do so on my own terms—another lesson Jonny has taught me.

I am laying claim to the sovereignty of my stories.

WHAT I HAVE LEARNED about academia is that it will accept you into its halls and classrooms, teach you about Gothic and Victorian and Medieval literatures, shower you in theories of feminism, queerness, post-colonialism—and yet it will continually demand of its BIPOC students that we write and defend ourselves into being. In doing so, we provide a primer in how to read our body and the bodies of our larger relationalities. Academia will require of its Black and/or Indigenous students a charter into our livelihoods, require a ledger explaining the legitimacy and applicability of our lived experiences and knowledges as having import for what already seems and feels like—and is—an overwrought and overdetermined field of whiteness and heteropatriarchy we call canon. I am full and burdensome to the point where I expunge and vomit out sentence, structure, and syllabic alike. I lay claim to my sovereignty through the repositioning of form, genre, story, and theory, condensing them more largely under the banner of being an otâcimow slinging biostory.

Being a poet, a novelist, editor, academic, and essayist—and having competed in these arenas of literature since the beginning of my post-secondary studies—I have become tired and bothered by these classifications, which I read as both boundary and border. Often, my prose is misread as poetic, my poems read as prosaic, my essays read as theory, my theory mistaken for biography. For example, the question I am most often asked about *full-metal indigiqueer* is: How should I read the work? This is a complex question, as I do not seek to pre-scribe meaning—by which I should say sound (as that is what is truly sought after, its sound)—to my text. Sometimes I'll joke: "Read it as boisterously as you'd like, just don't read it in a poet's voice." I say: "Feel the flick of a consonant on your tongue, shotgun a verb into being—speak story into liveli-hood." When I say "sound," what I really mean is orality. And what I mean in writing this here is that orality is reality. Orality is a sign plump with meaning: first, because it is a sovereign hook, lacing me into those bingo-hall snagging stories, or the tutelage of storying in my grandmother's house, where every woman from within a two-kilometre earshot one-ups the other in humour or tragedy around a slab of bannock and a kettle of Red Rose tea; and second, because orality never asks to be condensed into singularity. Rather, it cascades into infinite registers across time, space, and geogra-phies. Maybe, then, I have begun this book in an incorrect fashion. To talk about orality here, in this moment, requires me to talk about the fall, not of God or Lucifer, but of Sky Woman plunging into water from a crack in the sky—by which I mean the Spirit World that holds a creation story of its own, so that this is but another singular moment in the larger schemata of Indigenous creationism. To talk about oral-ity is to talk about history, to talk about history is to talk about concatenation, to talk about concatenation is to talk about language, and to talk about language is to talk about sound.

Can sound be given a history?

In her book *Memory Serves*, Sto:lo storyteller Lee Maracle details the role of orality within Indigenous ways of being, writing, and storying. She announces that "the language of poetry lives in the body and we are always hungry for it." When I speak of bodies, I open this noun's meaning into its playgrounds, the language of poetics, through which we may also say stories, all existing within and upon the noun's flayed innards: our bodies, bodies of land, water, literature, community. But this leads me to another question: What is the history of the poetics embedded within such embodiments? Again, I must turn to the beginning and defy any logic of linear plot within this book: we return to creation. "Our memories stretch back thousands of years," Maracle notes, "but we don't think about them until the condition for the use of memory ripens and calls us to remember." If story is the encasement of memory, then the stories of our bodies, our hunger for such poetics, is one rooted within the paradigm of the ancestral—and orality, then, disrupts any condensation of time into what we simply call the "present." My elders tell me that when we set foot on a piece of land—again, a body—we simultaneously experience past, present, and future. Temporalities sing harmoniously beneath the print of our soles, tinkling through bone and membrane. The land is an archive, is a library, is a genealogy—a body of land *is* a body of literature. Water remembers, it maintains memories, it recalls the substances it has previously dissolved; trees remember, and in their wounds is a witnessing of wars past, diseases eradicated. If the land can witness, it too can listen. And it talks through what we might call living stories: the way a tipi ring would point to hunting grounds; the way a waterway directs one to community or home; the way a petroglyph enlivens communal and historical dialogue.

I turn to my linguistic system to attempt to answer myself. In nêhiyâwewin we do not gender objects the way French or English do. Instead, we have animations, which differ from the aforementioned languages because we hold our relations within our languages. Where English would call a river, the sky, fire, a rock inanimate, nêhiyâwewin considers all of these to be animate beings imbued with spirit, kin to us. The non-human, the four-legged, the winged, insectoid, fungal aquatic—all of these hold space, relevance, and importance within a circular way of being in relation to each other, rather than a hierarchical model that positions humankind on the highest register. For this we say wahkohtowin, which translates to "all my relations," a term that many prairie Indigenous languages share, but more specifically denotes the act of being related and in relation to each other. Here, wahkohtowin is a means of existing within continuums, parallaxes, or in the wholeness of a circle. Ultimately, it is upheld through the active practice of what we call miyopimatisowin, or "the good life"—being in good relations and adhering to nêhiyaw laws of accountabilities to all our kin. As such, miyopimatisowin is kin to wakohtowin. nêhiyâwewin centres and privileges accountabilities and ethics within every speech-act we utter. Stories, the original and the contemporary, braid together wakohtowin and miyopimatisowin through the active teachings of embodied modes of being in relation to land, water, sky, non-humans. A creation story or a trickster's tale are active engagements with these concepts and are naturalized in the poetics of pimatisowin, the registers of life/living. As Maracle argues, "poems move people from where they are to where they need to go to ensure community development." In this way, the original and the contemporary understandings of pimatisowin actively engage accountability, an ethics of orality, and relationality through the mending of, and adherence to, Indigenous—here, specifically nêhiyaw—modes of governance. The poetics of pimatisowin are embodied through an engaged orality that is entirely about the wellness of the whole. Indeed, the very act of putting breath to language, of making sound, is an entry into community-based care. Orality, by which I mean a tool of storytelling, is therefore an entry point into community enrichment and the building of futures through the interlacing of our histories.

I would argue that words, orality, sound itself are kin to us since we not only breathe animation into language, but we also enliven stories through the deployment of our voices, senses, bodies. The act of speaking summons words into being through an entanglement of experience, memory, and recognition. And stories become communal through a schematic of ethics that holds us accountable to our relations; here, our words themselves become these animate kin. In this way, stories play a key role in the development, empowerment, and futurity of Indigenous peoplehoods. wahkohtowin is enacted again precisely because storying is directly aimed at community development and health—something, I would argue, that differentiates Indigenous stories from European literatures, which are so often consumed in a solitary fashion.

I WILL STATE HERE that although it is against my protocols, and at times feels voyeuristic, to be theorizing about Indigenous ways of storying and orating for the sake of easing the consumption of my own work (in fact, it feels like bringing a camera into a sweat lodge)—I do so because English as a language and form, and genres as subsects of writing, has continually failed me. In fact, English has harmed me and my stories through acts of classification, demarcation, and analysis—squeezing story into paradigms that often forcibly remove limb and tooth from my story's perceived burdensome and feral aesthetics, which defy and cry against the expected layout of genre. How do I theorize story? And am I the correct person to dissect our nêhiyaw concepts of otâcimow? No. But I am doing so in order to make sense to myself of just what I am doing in this blood-letting on these pages.

I have transfigured my definitions of what I am trying to do in this work from creative non-fiction to theory to essay to biotext—and ultimately found all of these an incorrect fit. Maracle asks us, "What is the point of presenting the human condition in a language separate from the human experience"? What does it mean to remove one's self wholly from stories; to write objectively as the inherent and sole truth-teller, as in non-fiction; or to delete pimatisowin from the autopsy of theorization? What does it mean to relocate and resize wahkohtowin from an engrossing, holistic circle into the rigidity of a peephole, that triage of objective theory? To remove story from theory is to remove the storyteller's body from the body of their text, is to move one into nothingness, into a "circle devoid of life," into the de-historicized Indigenous "was," into the closed loop of a zero. To erase, to remove, to calcify for the sake of academia, exegesis, primer, or publication is to rot in archive and pixel. "By demanding that all thoughts (theory) be presented in this manner in order to be considered theory (thought)," argues Maracle, "the presenter retains the power to make decisions on behalf of others and the gate is shut to ordinary citizens who seek to gain control over their lives." The closed circuit of theory being legitimized through objectivity and evidence is a horrific bloodletting indeed. Dare I drain the page of ink and blood for the sake of making a bound literary cadaver for inspection? The stasis of an exegesis removes me, the storyteller, from the rivers and canyons of my story's body— and demands that I hand over the key to such sovereignties to institutions and their purveyors. This is why I refuse "theory" as a nameplate for what I am attempting to do in this book. Bodies exist within their own multiplicities, and the body must stay within its bodies in order to maintain the sovereignty of story.

In *Shapes of Native Nonfiction: Collected Essays by Contemporary Writers*, Elissa Washuta and Theresa Warburton chart dozens of Indigenous writers and attempt to redefine what non-fiction might and ought to look like for Indigenous writings. They accomplish this task by likening their collection, and the stories within, to the crafting of a basket. Both note:

> The basket. The body. The canoe. The page. Each of these vessels has a form, a shape to which its purpose is intimately related. Each carries, each holds, and each transports . . . [T]he craft involved in creating such a vessel—the care and knowledge it takes to create the structure and shape necessary to convey—is inseparable from the contents the vessel holds. To pay attention only to the contents would be to ignore the very relationships that such vessels sustain.

Washuta and Warburton's editorial layouts are a stylization against anthologized literary productions of Indigenous non-fiction, which is far too often read, in a settler colonial misnomer, as representing a solidified Indigenous past. To relegate Indigenous non-fiction to the past is to create and foreground anthropologic literary expectations of the contours of Indigenous non-fiction storytelling. It suggests a desire for cultural authenticity on the part of the storyteller and their communities, and it crafts a spectral essence that we can never achieve, a type of ethnographic reporting, native informing, archaic spectrality. I see this in the so-often-expected Indigenous trauma narratives, which are now primarily residential school experiences. As Indigenous literatures attempt to move away from the over-determined but very real history of residential schools (I am writing this in the time of the Kamloops 215—the discovery of bodies of Indigenous children at the residential school in that town), the literary elites continue to reward and recognize contemporary narratives of these schools. While I am happy for the winners of these awards and accolades, what this narrative focus tells me is that these stories are still largely thirsted after by non-Indigenous readerships, and such a thirsting does not allow for stories that move beyond—as much as we can do so, given our own intergenerational traumas and survivals—the paradigm of this traumatic narrative. Perhaps what we can look for and see instead is, as Washuta and Warburton suggest, not simply the vessel as a utilitarian form, meant to teach and/or to inform, but rather as transporting and transformative kin that houses its own relationships, its own sustainability. We can think of a story as a basket, as a body, canoe, page, and living, breathing kin through the passing down of its oralities, or through the lived experiences of the writer's sharing.

Both Washuta and Warburton conceive of Native non-fiction stylizations as "an exquisite vessel," observing:

We conceive of the essay as an exquisite vessel, one that evidences the delicate balance of beauty and pain. The "exquisite" character of this vessel invokes simultaneously an exquisite work of art and the exquisite ache . . . By bringing to the fore a focus on form . . . we use the term *exquisite vessel* not just to name the work . . . but to draw attention to form as a creative and literary practice of reverence for the exquisite in its most literal sense of something carefully sought out. To *essay* is to try, test, and practice. The form of the essay, then, is a fitting site for the experiential and sometimes painful work of seeking answers . . . [T]o write nonfiction is to render experiences, memories, observations, and interpretations through prose, a process necessitating writer agency and allowing for emotional depth and transformation—not only of the narrator figure but of the writer who essays.

What I take of this for myself as an otâcimow is in the flaring intersections of art and aching. It is in this overlap where I posit my stories as an umbilical space between the body of text and the body of the writer, and furthermore, as woven from the surrounding larger bodies: the basket as a body of land that holds a body of water—which is to say that the stories I produce herein are a body of text umbilically tied to the exquisite ache of my physical body, which is bound within the cuppings of Treaty 7 and Treaty 1. Moreover, the process of storying becomes not only conversational with and from communities but also a conversation of and with the self: as the narrator detangles and informs themself of their own wandering questions, so too does the writer. Still, I cannot fully call my work an exquisite vessel. As posited by Washuta and Warburton, this transportation and transformation is done solely for the form of non-fiction, even if that form may include elements of the poetic or prosaic or biographical. As well, their ideas about the basket as a material and metaphorical mode of organizing and writing an essay that may be considered exquisite references an art technique that is foreign to my own prairie and woodlands understandings of my Indigeneity.

I turn instead to Lee Maracle's descriptions of orality as "spiritual concatenation," which she figures "between poet and listener is quintessential to the articulation of oral poetry, and the poem's achievement of this concatenation rests on the spirit." Concatenation, or "to link (things) together in a chain or series," is perhaps a more academically inclined theory of wahkohtowin. Interconnectivity, wholeness, and relationality are all bound up within her deployment of concatenation. But what does it mean to be spiritually concatenate? If words, through orality, are animated into being, then they too are imbued with spirit, are kin, as I have argued. And, as I have noted already, such forms of relationality require sociality. The role of the orator becomes one of sharing meaning and presenting the human condition in a language that is embroiled in the human experience. I have often said that I am not the sole author of my stories. I envision Indigenous oratories in my writing by recognizing the fact that I do not write in a vacuum, and nor do I think of storytelling as a solitary act. Rather, I am both the creator of, and the listener to, my own stories, making applicable and relevant my own knowledge as a means of laying claim to my own body, making sovereign my stories.

But am I able to braid my stories and storytelling into an explicit orality? To do so feels as though I am romanticizing my understandings of Indigeneity, as an Oji-nêhiyaw person, as a non-fiction writer, as an urban Indigenous person, and as a Two-Spirited person—one who is continually deferred into the past by Indigenous and non-Indigenous peoples alike, locked in the "was" of the Indigenous contemporary "now." Washuta and Warburton observe "the outmoded idea of Native non-fiction as nothing but a transcription of something that could have been or was delivered orally." I am cognizant of the ways in which anthropologists, writers, and social scientists too hastily wrote, and still write, about Indigenous lives auto/biographically as a means of preserving the vanishing inevitable. I am aware of the ways in which consumers of Indigenous stories have read, and continue to analyze, Indigenous literatures as testimonies to a vanished and forgotten "was" of Canadian and American history. Furthermore, as Stephen Graham Jones (Blackfeet) warns Indigenous non-fiction writers in *Shapes of Native Nonfiction*, be "prepared for people wanting to read this innovation as a callback to the oral tradition or an appeal to a different aesthetic." So, while the aesthetic of form and genre may change, as Jones notes, the audience, whether a reader, a publisher, or the academy, does and will read the work as a means of invoking the settler colonial imaginary of Indigenous literatures as romantic and idyllic.

. .

I THINK ABOUT ORALITY as testimony—because it is so often
read as such in our contemporary moment. And I find I must
unpack my difficulty in positioning my stories as strictly and
simply oralities.

Testimony is a powerful mode of witnessing and listening,
and one that we have deployed often since the publication,
in 2008, of the findings of the Truth and Reconciliation
Commission (TRC) here in the place we now refer to as Canada.
More recently, on May 27, 2021, the Tk'emlúps te Secwépemc
uncovered the remains of 215 children buried on the grounds
of the Kamloops Residential School in British Columbia,
sparking national movements of mourning and grief across
Turtle Island. Since then, the remains of 104 children have been
found in Brandon, Manitoba, 38 in Regina, Saskatchewan,
35 in Lestock, Saskatchewan, 180 in Carlisle, Pennsylvania,
751 in Marieval, Saskatchewan, and 182 in Cranbrook, British
Columbia, bringing the current total (which, we know, will only
increase in the months to follow) to 1,505 found children
who experienced genocide at the hands of the Canadian and
US governments' residential and boarding school colonial pro-
grams. This is in addition to the 4,100 already found through
the TRC—and these seven additional sites are but a small part
of the larger pool of recognized residential schools (not includ-
ing day schools, or the contemporary translation of such schools
into the Department of Child and Family Services). As of now,
the Canadian federal government has completed and/or imple-
mented only 10 of the 94 calls to action set out by the TRC.

I therefore find fault with the idea that the act of testimony is a transformative mode of empathy through storying—especially given its audience and use: settler colonization. I distrust the role of testimony within the era of the TRC for two reasons: first, who is allotted space to testify—that is, primarily Indigenous heterosexual cisgendered men; and second, the popularization and expectation of Indigenous residential school trauma narratives by publisher, reader, and the academy alike. The braiding of who is allowed to testify with narrativized trauma expectations has created a dangerous and disempowering mode of being for Indigenous women and Two-Spirit peoples. I find fault in this synchronicity: I fault residential schools broadly for the current state and livelihoods of Two-Spirit, femme, Indigiqueer, and Indigenous women across Turtle Island who are affected profoundly by Indigenous men, masculinities, and heterosexualities. I observe the ways in which residential schools enacted harm physically, mentally, spiritually, and sexually against children and survivors of these schools, and specifically spotlight the role of same-sex sexual assault as an expansive tool in continuing the dehumanization and demonizing of queerness, transness, and Two-Spirit identities. That dehumanization is thus further entrenched within Indigenous epistemologies, and we are further sidelined as, continually and sluggishly as Indigenous and non-Indigenous peoples, we try to rectify the trauma of residential schools. As we glacially centre and heal the pain of primarily heterosexual cisgendered Indigenous men, we unfortunately sideline

Two-Spirit people and Indigenous women. I find the role of testimony, through orality, to be a powerful enabler of this vulnerability, given the optics, hungers, desires, and idealizations of non-Indigenous purveyors and voyeurs who latch on to these narratives as absolutes.

But nothing is absolute. I might try to call this book creative non-fiction, memory work, orality, biotext, or an exquisite vessel—but I lack the ability to move into public histories, not only as an Indigenous person but also as a Two-Spirit person, for such histories have been so carefully and politically removed or destroyed, or, as with the Catholic order that ran the Kamloops Residential School, an authority has outright refused to share familial and historical records. To move freely into a space of history, whether public or personal or familial, is sometimes to move into a rupture that is beyond and outside of space and time, into a wound, which is its own place, albeit an archive not easily accessible or available, and sometimes more damning.

I find myself yet again in a hinterland of dislocated meanings. If not orality, memory working, non-fiction, exquisite vessels, or biotext—then where am I to turn for the name of what I am writing? I find myself in a state that Daniel Heath Justice, in his text *Why Indigenous Literatures Matter*, calls the "crushing weight of possibility unrealized." I strongly and wholly attribute this state to the loss of the lives of our children in residential schools, and to the larger system of settler colonization upon Turtle Island. For if I was able to move freely into and between personal and public histories, this naming of the genre of this book might have simply been solved by asking my nôhkomak and môsomak. Justice asks us to be wary of "includ[ing] ancestors [as] targets of expropriation, exploitation, and destruction. This targeting is literal as well as figurative."

It's here I find myself bewildered by how I call myself an orator, a memory worker, and/or even an exquisite vessel. As someone without an upbringing, as a child, in nêhiyaw epistemologies, languages, cultures, or protocols, I have had to seek out and autodidactically inform myself about information that should have been accessible to me, if not for the genocidal practices of settler colonialism. I have been wary of romanticizing or politicizing ancestors for the sake of clinging to a knowledge I can transform to meet my own requirements of being, living, and surviving as an Oji-nêhiyaw, Two-Spirit person, and otâcimow. Justice observes that "ruptures, too, can be read. The absences tell stories of their own," and notes that the "archive is both an imperfect tomb and site of resurrection. For now, it has to be enough." I have learned that I too can enact lateral violence, even as someone who is profoundly injured and injuriously lost, by deploying nêhiyâwewin and reading backwards, attempting necromancy in order to find and cling to kin I can call a Two-Spirit storytelling ancestor. Like the writers cited by Joanne Saul earlier—Wah, Kiyooka, Marlatt, and Ondaatje—and their biotextual writings, I too am on the peripheries of belonging, an outlaw, an outcast, an outsider to my own Indigenous and nêhiyaw communities lost in the rubble of excavation and removal. Like them, I too am working within the rupture, within the wound, wayfinding in the absence of stories, engraving on the walls of a tomb that simply has to be "enough" for now.

What does literature mean to someone who is disbarred from his own storytelling histories? What does literature mean to one who is also disempowered in the formulations of its academic pedagogies? "'Indigenous literature,'" Justice writes, "two powerful words in a powerful relationship—but not a neutral one . . . [F]or some readers, these two words together are an oxymoron." For so long, Indigenous literatures have been disallowed from the capital *L* of literature for being primitive, premature, and/or not yet developed enough to be experimental in form, genre, or aesthetics—and yet we are, and have been forever, storytelling in all forms as a means of proclaiming, testifying, and orating that we are, were, and *will* be here. Justice, quoting Robert Warrior (Osage), states that "nonfiction has been for more than two centuries a primary means through which Indigenous people . . . articulated their experiences of modernity." I wonder: Is Indigenous non-fiction both a means of archiving for Indigenous peoples while also being a tchotchke for non-Indigenous consumers? Yet this book, to me, is wholly an attempt to remove Indigeneity from the prison house of the "then" and release it into the "now."

Indigenous storytelling deploys all genres and no genres simultaneously, as it envelops past, present, and future seamlessly. What does realism mean to Indigenous literatures when what it wholly regards as real—dreams, tricksters, ancestors, visions, anthropomorphism, little people, star people, wendigo— is disregarded as speculative or fantastical by other readers, publishers, and academia? How can our stories become "literature"—assuming we even want this—under the colonial, classed, and heteropatriarchal gatekeeping of form and genre? When I write of maskwa and nanabush in *Jonny Appleseed*, this is most often read by non-Indigenous audiences as a reinforce- ment of settler colonial ideologies of Indigeneity as flora and fauna. I suppose I mean to ask: What is the use of realism in Indigenous literatures when its realities are misinterpreted as fodder for idyllic and frontier fantasies?

I side with Justice strongly in his concept of "wonderworks," although I do not quite find it is the fit for me as a prairie, woodlands, Two-Spirit Oji-nêhiyaw. But I observe his argu- ment that:

> . . . the assumption of a singular model of "realism" as the dominant standard against which literary merit is measured is problematic, especially for those minoritized communi- ties whose alternative ways of engaging that reality don't always fit smoothly into the assumptions of Eurowestern materialism . . . Privileging this narrow definition of literary realism can actually work violence against our struggles for figurative and experiential liberation, for it presumes, first, that there's a singular reality against which all others must be compared, and second, that any cultural expressions or

understandings inconsistent with that interpretation are deficient at best, pathological at worst . . . [W]hen "realistic" fiction demands consistency with corrosive lies and half-truths, imagining otherwise is more than an act of useful resistance—it's a moral imperative.

THERE IS SOMETHING grand in this mission I have set for myself—in thinking about this anglicized placeholder, these Indigenous biostories; in wanting to find and define a field of literariness that fits the multiplicity of identities that I house and hold dear; in attempting to find a canal in which to place my kayak and paddle the currents of Indigeneity, mental health, and queerness in a single stride instead of relying on the motoring of machine. Yet I am not seeking to write a grand nêhiyaw tragedy. Rather, I seek a grand mode of transformation. I posit my storytelling against the boulder in the waterway, the singularity of "realism" as a dominant aggregate in the wake, a change of current in the eddying. I can no longer afford to privilege the narrowness of "literature" when it comes to defining and laying claim to the sovereignty of my stories—for they are not solely mine, they are ancestral, communal; they are of the living and the dead; they are of aggressor and lover; they are of child-me, elder-me, present-me; they are wondrous, indeed, in their housings. I dare myself to dash through the definitions of genre and form, to enact decolonization, turn it from simply a definition into animated verb—for, if I am to defy national boundaries and borders of nationalism and Indigenous nationhood, I must do it here on the page too, bound within spine and glue. I must imagine otherwise towards a horizon of richer possibilities, brighter utopias for me and the kin I am accountable to, for the children and youth who will follow in my wake.

Recently, I was sitting on a literary board. During our meeting, another member rated my BIPOC selections quite low, noting that he could not comprehend the "narcissism" of these writers who were, to him, so self-indulgent and revealing of themselves meta-narratively as both speaker and author. He called the books I selected "character studies" and "without plot, only character driven." My rebuttal was that we cannot call—and I used the term "biotextual" then—the writing of BIPOC writers who may be fusing themselves with their characters narcissism or character studies under the larger system of white supremacy. This member announced, "This is about writing, not politics, Josh," and I responded, "The fact that you think writing is devoid of or annexed from politics tells me everything I need to know."

This conversation has stuck with me, for it told me two things. The board member's comments informed me that Indigenous literatures are seen as "juvenile," even if they are award-winning and widely celebrated; and that the state of publishing and award culture upon Turtle Island is rapidly shifting to include and celebrate BIPOC and queer voices, and not wholly centring the experiences of white, heterosexual, cis-gendered men whose stories may be read within the dominant aesthetic of realist fiction. What his projected anxieties, riddled within his comments, told me was that Indigenous jurors and literatures have no place within the arenas of literary excellence, by which he meant white excellence; that our stories are simply nostalgic takes on a "was" or a "before" that preceded the impact on us of the inherent and lived trauma of colonization; and that when we do succeed, it is only because of affirmative action for the sake of inclusion—by which he meant to say that Indigenous literature, at its finest, is simply pulp fiction and fantasy.

Justice, too, speaks on this topic of the deficiency inherently attributed to Indigenous literatures and stories. He announces that:

> [If] the colonial imaginary is predicated on a fiction of Indigenous deficiency and absence, an empty frontier awaiting white supremacy to give it shape and substance, then what alternative does the escapist Indigenous imaginary offer to us as readers and as bearers of story? How might a different way of engaging our histories and imagining our futures chart a different course for relationships and difference possibilities for the future?

It is here where I find myself in this impasse, or rather wondrous oasis, of being both linguistically lost yet infinitely open to redefining how I attribute my stories as "literature." Without borders of genre or form, we reclaim the sovereignty of story, the orality of voice, for richer soils of decolonization— and can posit ourselves as ancestors in the making, while ancestrally speaking too. We are inheritors of story, even when these are found in the wound or the rupture, and our concepts of temporality posit us as speakers to that which we might consider the dead or forgotten. We are forever positioned in the rich membrane between material and immaterial worlds. This is a key concept I take from what Justice calls "wonderworks": the attempt of wonderworking towards that whole, even when forked and fragmented onto a path I must walk to find my footing as an otâcimow. "Indigenous wonderworks are neither strictly 'fantasy' nor 'realism,' but maybe both at once, or something else entirely, although they generally push against the expectations of rational materialism." Justice offers wonderworks as a means of working within the rupturing fabric of colonial literary nationalisms and Indigenous decolonial sovereignties, in terms of place and story, form, and genre. Within the noun of "wonderwork" emerges a beautiful bricolage of intersecting storying—what we might even call genres, in that fantasy, speculative fiction, horror, realism, and poetics enmesh and embroil when cauterized by the speaker's own Indigenous epistemologies.

"Wondrous things are *other* and *otherwise*," Justice writes, "they're outside the bounds of the everyday and mundane, perhaps unpredictable, but not necessarily alien . . . but not necessarily safe, either. They remind us that other worlds exist." What a delightfully queer way of seeing oratories and storytelling. Like the biotextual writers Saul invokes, like the exquisite vessel of Washuta and Warburton, like the moving oralities and hungry languages of Maracle—all are adamant in their desire to embrace what we might call this otherness and mutate into non-ness, into not being able to be defined, located, mapped, or transfigured onto literary nationalisms or literal nationalisms. How wondrous the rupturing between the boundaries—the bounds of the everyday and mundane, borders of genre and form, between this world and the next, of ancestor and star people, living and dead. It's in the embrace of a glimmering edge on the sheer fabric of other worldings—by which I also mean wordings—that our stories challenge, upend, and serrate the safety of what was otherwise thought of as canon and singular models of literary realism. I ache for it to be known that the presumptions of reality within a settler colonial imaginary are in fact *the* fantastical; that the building of border and boundary around form and genre, the prescription of these enmeshments upon our stories and storytellers, is and was a means of entrapment and caging—I howl at the gate of these partisans.

I do not know if I yet have a word that I can solidify and consolidate as *the* word for a wonderworking, boundary-defiant, biotextual, temporally oral, Two-Spirit exquisite vessel that is grounded within a nêhiyaw epistemology—I am still reeling in that rupture.

I Own a Body
That Wants to Break

MY SISTER AND I share secret conversations. We talk about the darker things in ourselves, desires, fantasies, what harms us, and the practices we've mastered to harm ourselves. Last week she had a panic attack, something that happens to her since the birth of her daughter and the postpartum depression she overcame, and suddenly she couldn't breathe as she sat on my parents' couch. My mother held my sister in her arms while my sister gasped for breath, reassuring her everything would be okay. I imagine my sister's breaths, those sharp staccato inhales, lungs aflutter in their bone cage, and the mind enacting its acute stress response, fight or flight. What does the mind fight against? What does it fly against? When I talk to my sister afterwards, she tells me she's stressed from school, from moving homes, from a new marriage, a new daughter. I want to tell her that at the bottom of all this is colonialism—we're all fighting and flying from that revenant.

My sister-cousin, too, experiences attacks like this in school. They cause her loneliness, depression, isolation, fear. She has suicidal inclinations, seeks out substances. And last month my cousin-brother called me one afternoon to tell me he wanted to die. We talked on the phone for well over an hour, me using my writing abilities, asking him to describe little details around him. What colour is the floor? Is it cracked? Is it darker in the corners? What kind of dirt do you think caused that? I then moved on to larger questions: Have you thought about what you'll make for lunch? What about dinner? Are your shirts clean for tomorrow? Oh yeah, which one do you think you'll wear? I felt as if I hijacked his mind, however briefly, to become his senses, to reel in the mind from its universal inclination to die by acting like a camera, zooming in on the minuscule, the smaller world, so that he could locate his self, feel grander, feel more present. He cried the whole time, telling me he loved me, and I returned the love. From out of a mouldy crack in the floor we blossomed into his traumas, observing how the world likes to break him, how he likes to break himself, how as a family we have normalized the rhetoric of destruction. I made him laugh, telling old stories from when we were kids, reminding him of how much he is loved, reconnecting the tendrils of story that tie him to us and to the land. And we both smiled. I could hear his smile on the other end of the line because his lips always twist into a knotted cherry stem in his dimples, causing his vowels to whistle. I told him I'd e-transfer him a forty so he could eat the next day, and buy a pack of cigarettes. Then I hung up the phone.

I ate pain like a glutton.

Even my mind felt heavy.

I put my cellphone on the counter and looked down at myself, my belly bloated with story and pain, my guts twisted, asking me to relieve them. I nodded slowly, resigning myself to this space of defeat, and walked to my bathroom. I raised the toilet lid, turned on the sink, wet my hands so as to lubricate them, rolled up my sleeves, and bent the body into a ninety-degree angle. I planted my legs like trunks and placed my glasses on the counter. I put four fingers into my mouth, rotated them as if I were a drill, and tickled my tonsils. The first gag is a dry heave, always, bringing up a droplet that is the promise of a river emerging. My finger reddened in its usual scarred spot just above the pointer finger's mountainous knuckle. After the first swirl, I knew my body was ready to cascade, finger dancing with tonsil as the body released its excrements. I continued this, in the usual habit of eights, until the burn erupted and my teeth felt like moss and my tongue acted of its own accord, pushing itself up to the roof of my mouth to suckle on saliva rather than stomach acid.

There are days when I run my hands over my body and feel beautiful, if only for a moment: the caverns of my belly button feel like the foothills, the knobs of my nipples like hoodoos, all pliable and fleeting, and the indent and expansions of my mid-section feel like the breadth of the prairies. There are days when I think back on my life as an overweight femme queer and tell myself: I'm here, even though the world told me I would never be. There are days when I look into the mirror and I see me in my entirety: ravishing, intelligent, accomplished, an ancestral nebula of light pounded from a star. I am told the formation of a galaxy, star-birthing, is the same process we undergo in the womb—that our formation is a mirroring of the other one. I remind myself in these downtimes that I am galactic in my wellness.

Then there are the days when I look at myself and feel like stretched muck.

Sometimes I enter this space in myself I don't like, this space where I walk around like a ruination, this space where I lose myself and become a receptor: I listen but never absorb, I smile while the tongue sings a death-song. You ask me where I go when I don't listen to you, and I say, with a crooked nod, "I'm here," even as I know, deep down inside, that I have left my body—I'm in a torture chamber of my own creations. I go into a space of myself where I've housed all my hurts and cradle them like babes. I feed them, but they are never full. I squeeze blood-milk from my nipples, I nurture wendigo as a relative. Sometimes those pain-babes offer me more than the world ever has. Sometimes friends who see old photos of me from when I was in my largest state of matter ask, "Who is that?" I joke that this child-me in the photograph, the boy with a smile as supple as an almond, is my dead brother, because he looks nothing like me now.

I cannot always tell if that is an ethical joke to tell anymore.

I see the destruction I cause in my relationships, platonic or intimate, and I watch myself sever that braid between us, because I become a ghost in those moments and you are a jack trying to access some current of me. I reassure you that I am not glum or unhappy. As a writer I feel I have mastered the ability to twist story, and I nod and lie down at the other end of the room, as far away as I can get from you.

I lose a bit of myself every time I do this, until now I feel I am a tattered rag.

I have always tuned in to music and lyrics when I enter this space, this netherworld. I am obsessed with the song "Creep" by Radiohead. I churn the refrain, "I want a perfect body / I want a perfect soul" in my mouth as if it were food, and sometimes I even guilt myself into believing I've consumed a calorie that needs purging. These are moments when even music makes me feel engorged. I love that song because I feel seen, perhaps, and because for three minutes I feel as if I'm in a world that doesn't judge me, simply asks me to be.

You are only the fourth person I've told about my eating disorders, and a part of me wants to apologize to you. I want to say: I'm sorry I'm weak, I'm sorry to enfeeble you, sorry I am not what you expected from me, sorry if I've fooled you into thinking I'm medicine instead of a carcass. I once told an ex-partner about my mental health after he asked why I had posted a lyric Instagram with a Radiohead quote. I said, I struggle with bulimia and anorexia; and he told me, "Beauty is in the eye of the beholder," as if that were a saving grace. He said, with confidence, I was what he wanted, needed, adored. Perhaps to a person not affected by mental illness, this would sound like reassurance, a key to the shackle I've tied myself down with. I nodded in return, giving him that crooked grin, and asked myself: What does it mean to behold? To owe? Who does the eye see, and where am I in that? What does that eye see, and why? Does seeing beauty imply an owing? Is confidence a benevolence or a violence?

If your body is fat, you are made aware of how it moves at an early age. You become aware of how your body betrays you in the cruellest of ways. You become aware of how you spill, leak, take up space, fill a seat, a room, the world. I used to frequent Tumblr websites that were coded as MIA or ANA for young teenagers, mostly girls, who shared tips on how to best manage weight through disordered eating. I learned so much from them: how to drink a glass of water before eating, two during, and one after, then wait five minutes to let your food become enveloped in fluid so that you can purge more easily; how to begin with a coloured food, like a red M&M or a piece of celery, so that you could colour-code the remnants of your stomach. I learned that bread is hard to purge but ice cream is easy, that the granulated sugars of candies will cut your throat but potatoes will come up like cream. I learned how to ritualize my eating so that I could fool those around me while also pleasing the anxieties in my mind that told me to rid myself of my *self.*

The first time I tried bulimia, I was fifteen. It was in the basement of my parents' housing complex on Outhwaite Drive in Manitoba. We had just eaten KFC, a rarity in our house, and my dad had ordered a Deep'n Delicious chocolate cake for dessert. My dear father, I love him so much—a child whose mother was murdered in the sixties; a child of the Sixties Scoop; incarcerated, a former drug addict, a man who knows self-destruction brought on by settler colonialism all too well. He always said to us, "Help yourself in my house and if you don't, you'll starve," making up for what I imagine were years of starvation and ruination, years of homelessness and juvenile detention foods, years of abuse and isolation. Food, to him, is an offering, a sign of health, abundance, community, love. He'd always tell me, "M'boy, if you're hungry, then eat," as if it would be an immediate and final act—as if this was always the last meal and we were on death row.

So I did. I ate because it pleased my father and my uncles, who would gawk at my large calves and say I was the next Bobby Orr, that my leg was a ham hock that could crack colonialism in half—that I was made from a bear who lived deep inside my Indigeneity. I liked how they approved of me in my largeness; me, a big Cree man who didn't take shit from anybody—they saw a weapon in me, one they never had access to, one who could fight back against the powers that had beaten them into feral wolves. Listening to them as they said this was one of the few times in my life I felt as if my femininity didn't overpower my masculinity, as if I was a man among the giants in my family. So I ate to please them, I devoured chunks of chicken, fries, coleslaw, and cake, and their smiles grew larger and larger. My father, I imagine, was filled with pleasure and reassurance with every bite I took. Here he was, a forgotten child who could provide for his family after emerging from the pit of desolation that the world had sentenced him to. I craved that smile.

Later in the evening, though, my belly rumbled, and the well of me became a swollen stream with a voice that called me beastly, hideous, fat, ugly. So I would go into the basement with my toothbrush under the pretense that I was going to use the new workout equipment my father had purchased. I brought along a plastic Walmart bag and set it up in the corner. I stabbed that toothbrush into my mouth and felt my tonsils jig a laborious dance. Up came chicken skin and glucose in a sludge of black goop, and from there the largest wave of relief washed over me and my stomach felt like a babe and the world felt all right again.

I crave your acknowledgement even as I write this.

I've been like this for thirteen years now. I first sought treatment when I was twenty-two, much to my own embarrassment. I had lost 120 pounds and was at my lightest weight—150 pounds, down from 290. My jawline glimmered in the sun, my arms were as slim as a pine branch, and everywhere I went I received copious amounts of praise. I was addicted; I am addicted. I have had conversations with my sister about this, talking about addiction, how it's intergenerational. We look to my father, that beacon in our lives, and trace his steps into substance abuse and drugs, and then his eventual overcoming of them. Addiction is hereditary, and mine just came in the package of disordered eating, tightly bowed and gifting me with thoughts that self-regulated my eating habits.

When I was twenty-two, I went to a walk-in clinic because I did not have a family doctor anymore. I saw a nurse and cried in her office, telling her that I had lost control of how I ordered my life. I flip-flopped between eating less than a thousand calories a day for weeks then eating something high in calories, manifesting a bulimic stage. Bulimia and anorexia are siblings, like those twins from *The Shining*, precursors to a wave of relief, always playing together in ghastly forms. They hold your hand and guide you into the deepest recesses of your psyche; they don't let you have your own subconscious, they make you sleep in their bed. The nurse asked me questions, made me take off my T-shirt to listen to my chest, and in that moment, I had never felt more ashamed. At my lightest weight, I lay upon her examining table and felt myself rush out from my own bones as soon as the shirt was lifted from my neck. I sometimes wish I had left my shirt there like a noose and hung from the rafters like the dead weight I felt I was. In that moment I cursed the nurse for not gifting me the grace to listen to my heart from underneath the shirt. I lay there as if I were a lake of grime, and she looked surprised. My nipples were lower than they ought to be, dark geysers among a tundra; my arms hung with wings; my love handles formed a comma on the table; and I had never felt more exposed, more weighed down by a body of grammar.

The nurse listened to my chest, took blood samples, asked me why I was there. This was the first time in my life I animated these words: *I can't feel myself anymore.* She, being a local drop-in nurse, had no real experience with my situation, so she recommended a clinic in Winnipeg that dealt with eating disorders. "It's a women's-only clinic," she announced, "but I can personally recommend you based on the fact we rarely see accounts of men with EDs."

It took me weeks to will the resolve to go. I did so one afternoon, after leaving class early at the University of Winnipeg. I told my professor that I would be unable to attend on account of a death in the family—a reason all too familiar to Indigenous students, for surely it was a viable one to white folks, and also, was I not attending a kind of funeral? When I got to the clinic, I sat in the lobby with women staring at me but smiling, and the burgeoning femme in me smiled back. It was a warm place, the women so gallantly triumphant in their pain. That was when I knew there was a spirit in me that could help, that understood what must be done, even if my visage still suggested "or . . ."

The physician at the clinic told me about eating disorders, how they're about control, about how the mind can collapse on itself, and the illusion of counting calories or purging them makes you feel as if you are containing a wilderness. She recommended I see a therapist to help me through the traumas that were haunting me. I agreed, and she set up an appointment, but

I never went because I was too afraid to talk to the spectres that cascaded through my bones and blood. What would I find? That I am another case of an NDN destined for death? What would the therapist say? That I inherit a death-drive whose pedal has been soldered down since 1492? Would she intercept this? Would I find that queerness is an objectification whose game I could never master? I smiled at the physician, promised I would go, thanked her for her time and her warming energy, and exited—but not before saying goodbye to the women in the lobby, whose lives were as much on the line as mine.

Through this visit I had reeled my spirits back into my body and set them at ease for well over six years. I maintained my weight, I exercised when I could—in fact I flocked to the high school track during summers in Selkirk in order to outrun the ghost of child-me, who was unable to finish a lap, and the wraith of my gym teacher telling me I was a disappointment. I ran five kilometres in under thirty minutes and felt accomplished, as if I were bench-pressing the gravity of colonialism in a single rep. For the first time, I didn't see the world pass me by; I passed through it instead, and the wind ran its bony fingers through my hair and my lungs were full of air, an element that loves to expunge itself. My breath was elemental, weaving through a labyrinth of cilia, lightly brushing my innards where my trachea makes music from inhalation, and hugging the cages of my body—much like how a diaphragm flattens into a stool that propels the world into my alveoli while my whole-body floats like a balloon. A single breath performs the entirety of one's life in the fraction of a second: I think of the way the body births life from a gasp, a gulp of the whimper from Sky Woman, and performs magic in the lungs. I give to my flora as much as I give to the world's flora; I expunge so that the trees may breathe again, as if we were throat singing to one another; I shotgun-kiss photosynthesis, and we perform cardiopulmonary resuscitation on one another, me and mistik—we are magicians, weavers, mystical in our make-outs, we cannot exist without one another.

I exhaled that long breath and continued running—the school backlit into an ominous thing so that I turned my head towards the sun, which pinkened on the horizon, and in its condensed light looked like a belly button illuminated by a flashlight. I laughed and blew it a kiss, feeling galvanized for the day. I had accomplished this feat that the world told me I could never do, my calves burning, my feet sore, my lungs asking me for rest.

Now I wait for snow to blanket the earth so I can story-tell you all this.

Tommy Pico asks "why the only thing more obvious than your body / is leaving yr shirt on in the pool"? I annotate a heart into the white space around this line of poetry, not because I love it but because the speaker and I share the pain that is shame. I have always dreaded the moment of stripping—and I feared nudity most in moments of intimacy. I have seen the eyes of partners, lovers, one night stands when they undress me and see the ways in which the body droops, where it is not tightened to the core, how their desire is tricked—and yes, I am a trickster of a man. By "body" I mean not only mine, I mean it here to signify bodies of land, water, literature. A body never meets the expectations of pornography—and by "pornography" here I mean terms of use, abuse, voyeurism, extraction, penetration; by "pornography" here I mean the machinations that consume and exalt accessibility. My body betrays my lovers as much as it does me, to the point that I wonder if I and everyone else are in a destructive relationship with the word "body" in all its morphologies.

Body means miyaw, while miyaw also means something that is given, he/she is given something, and corpse. I look to its roots, for the word "body" also comes from Middle English's bodig or bodeg, meaning trunk, and again this blanket of flesh is rooted in the land; I wear my skin ceremoniously, or at least I try to. The body is also the principal thing, the main part of anything, which itself, as a definition, comes from Old High German's botah, a word that has wilted into linguistic oblivion and bloomed into Leib and Körper. It's only in English that the *body* remains a great and important word.

Why, in nêhiyâwewin, is the body a gift?

I think that the body, too, is like a jack: with it, we plug into the womb of our mother and gain vantage points into the world that sits beside ours, or above, or sometimes below—which isn't to say I look towards Heaven or Hell, but rather that I look upwards into nôhkomak and downwards at nikâwiyak. Those are her breasts and there is her vulva—and looking in any other direction is peeking into kin. Our bodies, that is to say our nêhiyaw bodies, are read in different tenors from English and Western conceptions of body; here I am an offering, and no small sampling of me will feast you, for you are not of the spirit world, you are part of the embodied one. My body is a gifting, something I must give you, something with roots in corporeality, which extends into corpses—miyâw means all of these things.

I want to see my body as miyawâtikwan, meaning it is a celebration, it is joyous. Like when I come to you in the night, nudge the bridge of your nose with my tongue, lick the wound that exists in your canyon, and ask you if you'll fuck me? You do. I queer my spine, which is to say I churn into the cypress, climb on top of you, tell you to give something to me. I want to taste the trunk of your body, want to feel like anything other than a corpse. You churn sap into me when you're done eating, feed me carbohydrates and electrolytes, and this is the lifeblood we share between us—it has never been a dead thing. Afterwards I feel an overwhelming need to thank you, not for loving me, which surely you do, but because I feel guilty for having ever asked you to fuck me in the first place. My body is an offering, never a choosing. miyawâtikwan becomes miyâwaham; we are simply passing by the waters and I am drinking in the light.

I'll try to repeat this ceremony tomorrow.

I steel myself to show myself—because I want to be touched, loved, fucked, I want to take, taste, titillate, I want to feel normal in my drives. I dread bathing and showering. I steam the glass walls of my bathroom to hide my body in the mystification of mist. I fear saunas, change rooms, swimming pools, and hot tubs—all things my kin enjoy. I want to walk into a room and say, This is my body and I damn well own it—but ownership twists my tongue and then language tastes like laceration. Sometimes, when I'm alone, I unclothe and tell myself that I am a body worth loving.

In the spring of 2019, I was in Los Angeles attending a conference of the Native American and Indigenous Studies Association (NAISA). Los Angeles in the spring is like summer to a Winnipegger, and I wanted to sunbathe and read *Corpse Whale* beside the rooftop pool of the hotel where I was staying. But on my first day there, I wasn't allowed to enter the pool area because someone had diarrhea in the water, and the stink that remained was so putrid even the chlorine couldn't kill it. I said, "I know a thing or two about stink, I'm just here to sunbathe." The security guard said, "I don't care what you know, the pool is closed today." "I know brownness as a partnership," and I walked away from him in that moment.

I returned the next morning at eleven, the birds cooing on the ledges, and removed my shirt, rolled my swimming trunks up to my thighs, and let the sun kiss, lick, and wound me how it pleased. I read poetry in my nakedness and let my body defy gravity as it intended to. There on the sunbathing chair I revelled in my majesty. Helicopters flew overhead and my nipples nodded at them; birds flew by and my carbohydrates rushed to my abdomen to listen to their song. I snapped a picture and sent it to my partner, saying, "Hey hon, I miss you," an areola sneaking into the aperture. I scrolled through Instagram, found a picture of me and all my friends looking ablaze in a group photo. It was then that I saw a DM from a friend of a friend, someone who used to text me at 2 and 3 a.m. I opened it and saw the comment, "Damn your friends are sexy." As I readied to type thanks, he added another comment: "Your friends all look amazing. What's it like to be the fat, weird one in the group?" I replied, "Success takes a toll on the body," and deleted his contact information immediately.

But the damage was done. The work of six years had been unravelled, and I lay atop the roof like a spindle of silk—and ain't nobody ever going to reel a spool of thread back together just the way it was. My mind came apart, unspooling over one of the largest cities in North America. My body atrophied under the weight of shame. I would never be the same. I put my shirt back on and went back to my room, and I was a ruined muck once again.

My body betrays me in bewildering ways.

Sometimes I text my Two-Spirit friends, "I need ceremony right away."

Sometimes I wonder where nêhiyâwewin exists, where it moves within the body?

I think of English as cerebral and nêhiyâwewin as kinetic; I move through language as it mutates in my flora. What does it mean when someone tells you, "Wow, you've sure let yourself go"? What does it mean to let go of the self? Does it imply an abundance more than a withering? Can the self be enfolded in its skin, and still lost? I turn to nêhiyâwewin and learn that to say "self" is to say tipiyaw awîyak wiyapoko. I fold myself into the language and unearth the word "tipiyaw," meaning personally, really, in person, and one's own; while "wiyapoko" opens into "wiyâpitam," meaning s/he scatters, mixes, tangles. Then to say "I have let myself go" becomes "niya ayâw pâkitin tipyaw awîyak wiyapoko niyahk." The English translation is similar, except here the words branch into other opportunities, other meanings, leaking semantically: I have let myself go churns into I have let myself scatter, I have let myself mix, I have let myself tangle, while also implying ownership over one's entanglement. In addition, "niyahk" opens up conceptions of time beautifully, meaning beforehand, ahead of time; it also pluralizes the "me" who is being let go.

I nestle myself in nêhiyâwewin when these words are slung at me. I let myself go into the hinterlands of meaning, and my body is boreal, meaning that to lose myself is really only to lose the "me" that you interpolate as fat, abject, as lesser than the "me" that existed yesterday, to which you've never been able to conjugate. To lose myself, to let myself go, is to branch off into the wildest kinds of savagery, where the body expands, loosens, tightens around bone, rejuvenates epidermically—which you sometimes call epidemically—and tangles with my spirits that feast in the body I have named becoming.

Can a body be sovereign if it is fat? If it is queer? Can a body be sovereign if you continually self-destruct it? These are questions I wrangle with in the mind as I count my calories for the day, staying beneath that meridian of 1,500, scanning barcodes on MyFitnessPal and becoming a conversion that moves between imperialism and metric systems—both of which fit neatly under the crown of republicanism. Sometimes I think of *terra nullius*, that colonial mantra that calls our homelands "no man's land" in policies and courtrooms; I try to take up as much space in the cul-de-sac of whiteness because for once I am not the dead end. I chew on sovereignty, meaning I break it into meaning that tastes like sugars that decay my teeth—state power, authority, supremacy, self-control. These are all things I lack in my life, in this body, on my body of land. My mental health is the sovereign of my body—see the crowns that sit haughtily on my molars? Even the pulp in my teeth is clear-cut, even my collagen is colonized.

In nêhiyâwewin, ownership translates into tipiyawesowin, which roots into tipiyaw—again meaning personally, really, in person; and tipiyak, meaning just about, well/barely enough. Ownership, tipiyawesowin, here tangles with "I have let myself go," or tipiyaw awîyak wiyapoko, so I categorize them together, that passive-aggressive comment now placed alongside sovereignty: beauty is in the eye of the beholder, and bodies are the I of the beholden. I cling to tipiyawesowin over "sovereignty" because its tenets of ownership feel reciprocal, accountable—not about possession in its entirety but about maintaining just enough, well enough. I take into consideration the suffix of "-win" in tipiyawesowin, which indicates that this word has been transformed from a verb into a noun. Ownership is therefore not a violent verb; it is a statement that mutates every time one announces it, a noun without properness in all of its capitalisms. niya tipiyawesowin, tâpwe, niyawâw pâkitin tipyaw awîyak wiyapoko niyahk: I own myself, truly, I scatter myself into my tangles. When my orthodontist tells me that I need a root canal and I ask why, he tells me there is an infection in the pulp. I laugh and say, "I've been chewing on sovereignty for thirty years." He doesn't get it. "Sugar," I say. "Whiteness is sweet." He smiles, thinking I've complimented him, but the pus is the real culprit because the acids have eaten at it. See: I too leak in the bone. "Extract the tooth," I tell him, "but I'm keeping the crown." This is how I lay claim to a body that wants to break.

My Aunties
Are Wolverines

I'M LISTENING TO Lady Gaga's "Joanne," thinking about why it has become a standard song of NDN karaoke: one need only replace the name "Joanne" with (fill in the blank) to participate in mourning the constant loss of kin we now call ancestor. "Joanne" is dedicated to Gaga's aunt, who died at nineteen from lupus, and I think it's one of the most beautiful songs ever written. I'm listening to it right now, nikâwîs, my auntie, and writing this for you—and I'm having a hard time staying composed. There have been times, more so of late, when I'll fall into the pit of this song and won't climb out for days. I can't tell you how many times the phrase "Girl, where do you think you're going" has rung in my ears, and I have collapsed. I do this in the shower often, as the water and the tears run down and blend into me, by which maybe I mean nourish me, because this is when you feel most real to me again: when those memories loop through me like a basket and I am held, softly, warmly, kindly beneath beads of water that animate me, make me living story. I write this now because I have never let you go, and I hope, nikâwîs, you'll stay with me as I go?

Sometimes I listen to "Joanne" when I go for walks on my own, because I need to think, in the bone hours of the night. I mourn in latitudes, slowly, widely. I mourn as the bough waits for its ice to melt from its branchlet, weighted down by a gravity foreign to its own. On these walks I remember you, nikâwîs, in all your beauty and razing. I walk through Forest Lawn, which everyone here calls the poor part of town but which I like, because the houses in their little nooks remind me of the housing projects we used to live in, across from one another, where brown and black kids screamed in delight and ran across the roads holding hands. I find you there in the fields waving at me, the sound of softball cracking in the distance, your hair caught in the setting sun, dancing and ablaze in fringe and quillwork. On those walks I pass birch trees in the night, spindles of mistik lit so softly they look like spiderwebs, their shadows cascading across me—and here, even in the crisp month of January, I know you hold me in the weaving of shadows, that inverse plane, that spirit world, and I meet you in the unreserved, that meek mink kiss that only snow can afford.

Did you know, nikâwîs, that birch are a pioneer species of tree, named so because of their ability to grow on uncolonized lands, like a hinterland, an ode wrapped up in the peeling of their paperskin? Did you know that birch trees are a monoicous plant, which means they bloom unisexually and bisexually? Did you know the word "monoicous" comes from the Greek, meaning single and house? What a divine sign, I think, a single house, bough a burlesque practice, fluid sexuality, wildly gendered. The birch's samara reminds me of your hair, nikâwîs, tied into its braid, housing masculinity and femininity in equilibrium.

Are you that birch tree staring down at me?

I constantly ask myself if all writing is a form of mourning. Sometimes I reread Whitman because I remember being a fledgling writer and looking to him as a type of queer idyllic idol with a utopic vision of language, and because I used to dare myself to multiply. Whitman celebrates himself, and I am forced to ask my own self what is celebratory about story? No one taught me in my creative writing classes exactly the type of labour writing, thinking, imagining, building would entail. Narrative is a type of strip show, sometimes of the body, but more so of the spirit-body. As of late, storytelling has required a lot of me—me, alone, in my office, splayed across my couch looking up into rows and rows of books. Sometimes nîcimos comes in, asks me what I'm doing, and the only words I can muster are, "I'm remembering." This may sound trivial, but in fact is a wholesome act. To say remembrance or remembering in nêhiyâwewin is kiskisiwin, the act of remembrance, which in turn reminds me of kisîw, that s/he is cross and guards his/her own young from harm. You, nikâwîs, guide me through those memories, astutely and minutely, letting me recall them at a pace of my own making; you find me in the dreamscape and open the archives ever so slowly. Even in writing this I feel that I am skinning the spirit of its flesh, which is to say its memory, and splashing it across the page as if it were a divination of blood—and I wonder: Can you read me as you would tea? If you spread me too thin, I crackle into a fine dust that skitters into the wind propelled from the push of your lungs. No one warned me that writing would take my family away from me. I don't yet have the ability to mourn those who have passed because I have been working: on story, readings, interviews, dissertations, candidacies, comprehensive examinations. And you may say that is my fault—and perhaps it somewhat is— but it is also your fault for demanding so much of me and giving so little in return. And maybe it *is* my fault for liking you so much, for wanting to dance, sing, laugh with you—all things I love. But I am reminded that too much love is some-times a sickness, so I sit here coughing up a kind of phlegm that tastes too much like literature. I often think of Clive Barker in the film *Hellraiser*, who gently notes, "No tears please, it's a waste of good suffering." What is a productive use of suffering if not mâtowin? I have tried to be attentive to what we may call the act of suffering, wîsakahpinewin, which hides the word "wisakahpiw," or s/he laughs so hard or rolls around. nêhiyâwewin instructs us: laughter transforms the sufferer.

I put my body on the line just to tell you this.

nikâwîs passed away on February 20, 2016, at the age of thirty-nine after having lived a paralyzed life for a handful of her final years. Her NDN name was Walking Bear Woman, or, ê-pimohteyin maskwa iskwew, and the irony of her name is not lost on me. Three years earlier, nohkôm nitanskotâpan passed away on January 24, 2013, at the age of ninety, and every year when her birthday passes by, I think of those ceremonial gatherings she held in her backyard where my uncles, giants unto themselves, would buckle into laughter and pick up their nieces and nephews and spin them around in the long prairie grasses. I have not yet had the chance to mourn either of these miwamaskawâtisiw iskwew because I have always had to work. I deal with their deaths slowly, on my own, because the world likes to work me to the bone. I wish I could go back and mourn as I ought to have: with my kin at my side, all of us holding each other and dabbing one another's faces with a Kleenex and telling stories that make us laugh until our bellies burst and our floras make life anew right there on the church floorboards.

But that is wishful thinking, and instead I cultivate my pain into a garden that I do not know how to cull into beauty. Sometimes, when I'm left alone, I creep into my bedroom and look at the obituaries—I crack under the pressure, and grief rushes into me like a great wave. This is how I have to mourn now: silently, alone, shattered, ragged. NDNs were never meant to be alone, least of all in a time of need. But I try to mourn this way nonetheless, because what are the ethics of a delayed mourning for my family now that they have healed and moved on, tucking away memories into their most precious places in the linings of their spirit-bodies? What are the ethics of my own mourning for my cousin-sister and -brother, whose mother left them far too early for them to know how to transform pain into love? There's a type of selfishness in my delay; edging pleasure is a selfish act, and so is edging trauma. So, I sit in my bedroom looking at the portraits of those who have gone, their miwasin nêhiyaw mihkwâkan, and I remind myself that there aren't enough kisses for me to seal back inside the bits of me that want to break and break and break. I miss my kin; but more importantly, I miss the me that they brought up.

I hate it when I have to come back to them for the sake of my writing because they're still speaking to me and I'm still listening, and I can't help but feel like a glutton for doing so. I shouldn't excavate them for the sake of singing story, but some-times I think: Maybe that's what pain is? I hope you can forgive me, my iskotêw iskwew, my kîsik iskwew, my me. Sometimes love needs to be ground in order for it to be grounded.

I scare myself when I let myself transform into this being, one who opens himself up to the dam without knowing how to swim; one who lets himself feel without knowing how to separate hurt from health. I'm here, but I'm not really *here*: I'm looking at myself from above, disembodied, seeing the righteous holes the world has blown through me, wâsaskotew ninâpês, kîsik nîmihitowin, all star decay and birth bundled into a body that sometimes wants to implode. And if I were to do just that, I know I'd ooze out a miasma of dangling particles, all wanting to be animated.

I play ambient music on iTunes to put myself into the mood of mourning because I sometimes need to be seduced by pain, led towards it as if it were an oasis in the barren landscapes of my cortex's fissures; and I look at pictures of my family and I hear my mama laughing, I hear my niece's high-pitched squeals, I hear my sister's belly rumble, and I think to myself: Why do you lead yourself towards annihilation? And I cry— maybe because I'm selfish or I'm too damned thick in the head to teach myself how to love myself after all these years; or maybe because I know, when I let loose, a squall of salt water will pour from my aqueducts and I'll spill an ocean that's been churning in me since 1492. Sometimes, it's when I'm in the water that I feel most beautiful.

IF TOO MUCH LOVE is a sickness, then so too is too much pain. I let myself float, unencumbered, sense-deprived, and look at my life as if it were a slideshow. I'm trying to find the kid in me because he is galvanized light, and I am just a shadow reflecting in the wake, not knowing if I'm swimming upwards or downwards. I make like a leech and hold on, because sometimes that's all I know how to do. I scare myself, because I so willingly injure my spirits. I'm a wendigo who eats himself to mourn.

You can't eat pain without also eating memory, and you can't eat memory without eating story; to eat the self is to eat community is to eat those very ones you shield from the world.

Sometimes I think of mourning as if it were a haunting. I think of Ed Warren in *The Conjuring 2* singing Elvis Presley's "Can't Help Falling in Love" while Lorraine Warren looks at him with such love, knowing full well this man will be her downfall, even as the kids sing along with glee. I am forced to ask myself if pain is a possession, even as I know full well the answer: pain always adds an apostrophe before calling my name. The Warrens teach us that there are three stages of demonic possession: infestation, oppression, possession. Sometimes, when I let myself feel, I am like a possessed doll, sitting and staring at pictures, by which I mean staring at myself. And afterwards, after the high, I fall back into a state of being that gravitates me towards the bed; and just before I wake, I realize I've been in bed for weeks, rising only when the stomach aches from acids. And when I wake at last, I smile up at the ceiling, singing, "I can't help falling in love with you." What does it mean to be possessed by pain, haunted by mourning? I've no one to blame but myself for entering a torture chamber of my own creation, yet I never do so willingly. Sometimes I wonder how to mourn ethically when I'm a peg in a tipi circle. I mean circle as in continuum, and continuum as in wahkohtowin, interconnected, entirely related. Does responsibility to the circle come with age? And if so, what does it mean to shut yourself off from yourself for the sake of those who are younger? I wish defeating the pain and the haunting were as easy as strapping myself to the bed and yelling, "The power of Christ compels you," or deciphering the name of the demon that swiped left on my life and shouting, "Valak," into the shadows of my room. Then again, I think all horror stories are about Indigeneity—there's always a hidden NDN in every horror film; hell, even old Pennywise has become that "Indian Thing," what with the missing and murdered children attributed to the nearby tribal village. I think of Maturin, that simulacrum of mihkinâhk, and understand that all of Turtle Island is a horror story in the making. Still, the turtle imagery comforts me when I'm sunken into myself: I picture Maturin spewing out the universe because of his stomach ache, and feel sorry that he choked to death by inhaling a galaxy. When at last I wake into a state of malnourishment, I ask for a glass of milk, knowing full well that NDNs are naturally lactose intolerant. I imagine that in that moment when the dairy meets my flora, I too will spew out life from all this pain, my excrement a type of exorcism, a universe posited in my esophagus, wretched me retching terra. And then I laugh, much to the dismay of those caring for me, because I regress into childhood when I'm surrounded by hurt.

When I think of child-me, I picture my auntie in her townhouse across from me on Outhwaite—the Selkirk housing project that we sometimes call Sesame Street because low-income housing always looks like Oscar the Grouch—and I hear her guttural scream. She throws open her screen door, a plastic ladle in hand, and we watch a scrawny man running down the block, barefoot and bare-ass, his face the portrait of horror as he's called a "goddamned curse." I think, "Now there's terror in the making," and I smile up at my aunt from the cement where all my brown cousins are drawing chalk dinosaurs and pretending to be raptors.

We used to play this game as kids, a game we called Raptor, this being when the movie *Jurassic Park* was popular. We'd curve our pointer and middle fingers into a sickle claw and chase each other around the neighbourhood, infecting others, who became our prey as raptors until only one survived and we all got to finally feast. You'd watch us from the back window, shaking your head and laughing to yourself—silently, it seemed to us, because we could see but not hear you in the window where you watched us kids thrive in our imaginations. Later, when we'd come in for water, you'd say, "The heck you kids doing anyways?" and we'd all laugh to ourselves, as if only we were in on the joke. We caught you once in the living room curving your fingers into that sickle. You noticed us and turned red-faced. "Sakes, mind your business," you said before bursting into laughter and hissing prehistorically. You looked at your hand, which now became a claw, and chased us up the stairs with that sickle, screeching the entire way. I remember your hissing, our shrieking, and you eventually catching us and prodding our bellies with a fierce tickle that made the house shake with laughter. The neighbours didn't care for our noise, and they banged on the walls. You went straight up to that wall and banged back, inviting us all to join you. "Eh, shut the hell up," you yelled into the wall, your hands cupped around your mouth, "my kid's got a right to laugh."

I think back often to us in that little home, I animate it again. My aunt tucks her long black hair behind her ears and smiles at me, that ladle waving like a drumstick, and she calls us over because she's frying up some farmer sausage. Her home always smells sweet, as if Tang were an air freshener to mask the smell of cigarettes. She has a Madonna music video playing on MuchMusic in the background. "Material Girl" bops with its synth beat and Madonna lounges in an all-pink room wearing a black leather romper with lace gloves underneath. She's on the phone while the camera pans to a diamond necklace laid in a bowl of popcorn. We only hear Madonna speaking on one end of the conversation, saying, "Yeah, he's still after me, he just gave me a necklace. I don't know? I think it's real diamonds. Yeah, he thinks he can impress me by giving me expensive gifts. It's nice, though, you want it?" The video then switches to Madonna in a Marilyn Monroe-esque getup wearing an all-pink dress, a blond wig, and that necklace draped around her while four men swoon around her with paper hearts. She knocks them all aside and descends the pedestal they've placed her upon. "Boys may come and boys may go / and that's all right, you see? / Experience has made me rich / and now they're after me" echoes through the tiny hallways of my auntie's housing project apartment. My auntie bounces in the kitchen, digging through her refrigerator, assessing her methodologies for stretching a five-dollar bill into a meal for seven—a practice she's mastered. She's wearing a robe, a set of pyjamas beneath, and her hair strung into the tightest ponytail as her black hair sways down her back.

What is it about Madonna that interested you so much, auntie? Was it that she was free, in all manner of sexuality, gender, and femininity? Was it that she could shatter the image of pink as meek and timid and splash across it leather and lace in all its boisterous volumes? Was it because you felt more comfortable in your masculinity than your femininity? While you scoot around that kitchen skimming for trimmings for lunch, I watch how you move through your household. You press your feet down hard, the balls of your feet knowing to pound so as to announce your presence. Your fingers are long but thick, nail beds chewed down, keratin a sheath. We never had much money and you had even less, but you took that lesson from Madonna, didn't you? Experience made you rich in life, taught you how to stretch a toonie into dinner, how to fend off men and summon the bears you housed, taught you how to balance your genders into a bodyhome that knew equilibrium. You have no way of hearing this, but I want to thank you. I gravitated towards you because you knew how to plunder iconography and animate your body however you damn well saw fit; I want to say thank you for being a lesson in comfort with one's gender, body, sex, sexuality.

Sometimes I play Madonna when I'm home alone, blasting the music so that her voice expands into every corner of my home, and I dance. Sometimes it even feels as if you're there dancing with me again, that awkward shuffle between mis-matched bodies, one child, one adult, hands latching and our feet aching to pound every ounce of our weights into the floorboards, let those neighbours know they ain't getting rid of us that easy. Before I know it, an hour has flown by, and when I finally open my eyes, my caruncle spills water, warmed from the swaying of saline in almonds they call lacrimal. I turn off the music as a new song starts and I sing with a giggle caught in my throat: "I hear you call my name and it feels like home." Those were among the first few moments I was intro-duced to queerness, when Madonna and her gaggle of gay men were voguing behind her. Thank you, auntie. (Nowadays, though, I correct Madonna: this ain't simply a material world, it's an immaterial one too. We made it through the wilderness, didn't we?)

Auntie's old frying pan flicks up beads of grease that would make any other cook shy away, but her thick brown arms steady themselves through the onslaught. Pain doesn't faze her because she has no business with hauntology. She slides thick sections of sausage onto our plates and drowns them in ketchup, then tosses forks our way and says, "Eat up, m'boys." We all join her on the couch and watch *The Price Is Right*, releasing a synchro-nized yell: "Oh for god's sake, you slack old thing!" Auntie tells us, "Boys, don't ever be the petty chump who bets a penny over the highest bidder. Everyone deserves a fair chance, you hear?" When one of us asks her who was that man running away from her porch, she says, "That old heatbag? Just some chump who can't handle a wolverine." When adult-me looks at child-me, I look back with foresight, knowing this one, my auntie, has numbered days, goddamnit. I think of the words I use to narrate her. What does it mean to be a raptor before her rapture? What does it mean to invoke terror in the name Terri, the name of my auntie? And why are my aunties wolverines?

Every year, on the anniversary of my auntie's passing, the family share online photographs and stories about her life, saying how much they miss her, how much they love her. This is an event that also always triggers a family member who is suicidal, and every year I wonder: What are the ethics of mourning and remembering, especially in hypervisible cyberspaces? How do you mourn without causing harm? I've been to my fair share of funerals and never once have I cried—I think of myself as a glutton that way; I eat pain the way I inhale air, my stomach is lined with prayer. But, like any well after a good rainstorm, you sometimes overflow, even to the point where the well screen cracks and pours back into askiy. These days I turn to nêhiyâwewin to help me understand this responsibility, because my body is beyond the point of bursting. I try to find a way of dealing with it within our linguistic and kinship systems. I ask: If relations are animations, then can you animate pain, make it kin? And, if so, can this pain, this kin, become something you make love to? I wonder: Can NDN affect be translational and transformational rather than simply transportable—must we forcibly apply our wounds into another? Are some people better at transforming than others? How do you heal harm without causing it?

All of nêhiyâwewin is simultaneously singular and plural, so I take it upon myself to think in terms of all my relations—because no one mends in singularity.

I take a lesson from my aunt: to be a raptor is to be prehistoric, while to be a rapture is to be futuristic. I learn from her that no one is ever really gone. She still teaches me when I stare at her obituary, when she wraps her webbing around me like a papoose, gives me stories from the birch tree. The body atrophies, it sags, it decays, but the spirits glow well beyond any type of settler temporality. Some say she is nowhere now, but I know nowhere is an everywhere. I have a good laugh at nohkôm for naming her Terri, which all white men always read as terror. A tiny nêhiyaw iskwew with a plastic ladle in hand is a fearsome warrior indeed; their blistering asses know that. When I'm possessed by pain, I take a lesson from child-me and invoke the wolverine, invoke my auntie.

The name "wolverine" comes from the Latin word gulo, meaning glutton; wolverines are ferocious hunters that can even take down a black bear. They climb trees and jump on their prey to hunt, and they have hunting ranges as extensive as one thousand square kilometres. They know a thing or two about sovereignty and about taking up space as a tiny body. In nêhiyâwewin, kîhkwahâhkêw means wolverine. I look for words akin to that, and I seek out language as I do my loved ones. kîhkâw means old person or an elder; kihkwahaskân means a grave, burying spot; kihkâm means to scold; and kîhkêw means to heal, to mend. Every language is a web of meaning, and I hold that to account here because I need my language to work, for my sake, and for theirs. When I sound these words out or say things like "holy hell," "heatbag," or "slack ass," the inflections instruct me. The vernacular, or the accent, tells me to listen to the rise and then the bounce of language through prepositions to the aural spike at the end; a sentence tells me that the slang we use is our language, only dormant, singing in sound—all of us who use it have access to its transformational elements. Wrapped up within wolverine, into which I now thread auntie, is the recognition of that which has passed, of the old and elderly, of knowledge, of discipline, but also of healing. To put this into further play, wolverines are also carrion, ones who eat dead flesh, gluttons—but here I don't think of them so much as wendigo but as ones who eat the dead: spiritual carrion, ones who take from me the parts that are decaying, the parts that break between my thighs when I walk, the hurt that has fallen off and rots in the sun. Maybe now I can think of my ancestral kin as those who eat pain rather than cause it—I just sometimes get my verbs mixed up. See: Auntie is a stalwart lesson in the making. I only need to listen, something I've never been good at—although I should practise, unless I want a spanking from a wolverine. My auntie is that wolverine, is a spiritual guide, is an ancestor who has never left me. And ain't that the grandest laugh?

An NDN laugh always seems to upset whiteness; settlers don't seem to understand that laughing is a type of coping. Sometimes I talk with my white friends when they're racked

with pain and tell them, "M'boy, you just need a good laugh,"
and they look at me as if I just salted their wounds. One time
I told my brother-in-law (who is white) that during funerals we
burst into laughter, and he took that as a sign of disrespect. Yet
laughter is an exorcism is a vial of holy water is the Ritual of
Chüd. After nohtawiy lost his kidney to cancer, my family
laughed in the ER. I think of laughter like a weaving, spelling
out magic, laughter being the animation of sakihitin but
stitched together into formation of a star, kisakihitin being a
live being, breathing through the breaths we share, holding us
tight, laughter like a turtle rattle, laughter more a creation story
than an end-stop—and whoever said we deployed such things
anyway? My kin once taught me to find my centre, my middle
of nowhere, my origin spot, where my first fibre of being was
weaved and suckled nutrients through a break, where I first
was kissed by fire and by women whose names all sounded like
wolverine, and to sing from there. They said, m'boy, just sing
from there. I always have the answers in me; lessons, like language, are never forgotten, just forgone.

So, where do I go when I'm not listening? When I was a kid,
the women in my life used to tell me to "quit feeling sorry for
yourself." What does it mean to be told to quit feeling sorry
for yourself? Does it mean I'm not a self worth feeling? Or that
I drape hurt like a shawl over myself? I don't mean to be extraneous about this, I don't hold the words as a badge to heighten my
suffering over yours—but, then again, maybe I do mean to be
extraneous. Suffering is a skin and I've wrinkled mine to show

you how it eats at me, how sometimes I need you to witness me. To feel sorry for yourself is to cradle a wound; to feel sorry for another is to pity them. I don't mean to pity myself as much as it may seem; I mean to purify myself. I think of suffering as I do a fruit fly: they are both attracted to fermentation, to the dead and dying, to decay, to sweetness, and sometimes all it takes is a soap bubble to kill them. These are natural processes of life, are they not? To be fed, to live, to feel pleasure, and to reproduce? Who am I to play kîse mânito and decide who or what is worthy of living and of dying? When I empty my jam jar full of apple cider vinegar and dish soap, I pour a grave-yard into the toilet—and it looks too much like emesis, so I churn into myself and thicken spirits into butter.

Maybe the point is not to rid yourself of hurt, because without it you cannot feel health; these days I think of hurt and health as a polyamorous couple where each one aches to be kissed in equal measure. If the body is a hoodoo, sandstone, I let the wind eat me as I cradle these spirits to my bosom and wait for us to be released. I believe that all of life collapses into these two categories of suffering and wellness, so I animate them as kin. The land and its elements are my aunties calling me home, into that centre point which is a nowhere, by which I mean a place that English has no words for, is an everywhere, is a bingo hall, is a fourth plane, is an ocean. The waves have placed me here only to wait for me to come to spirit-home; my job is only to nurture myself in all my haughty emoting until

I emerge full-fledged and fully rounded. kinânâskomitin nikâwîs, my auntie, my mother.

"EVERY PART OF MY aching heart needs you more than the angels do" is a line in "Joanne" that sticks with me everywhere I go. I hope I'm not selfish in writing this, auntie, but I grasp so tightly onto this photo album I've crafted because I sometimes fear that letting you go will let me go—and I don't have the capacity to let go of that tiny world you've nestled into me. I also don't want to say "never go," or that I could possibly need you more than any spirit would. I only sustain my need for you because I haven't fully dealt with your death yet. I want to say I'm sorry I couldn't make your funeral, I hope you don't take it as a dishonesty. This, here, is the wildest kind of honesty I can muster. nîcimos tells me that I need ceremony, need to talk to an elder to help deal with this grief, but you and I both know, as urban NDNs, it ain't as easy as going out to the bush with a bundle of sweetgrass and a pouch of tobacco and finding that ceremony readily available—we both know things don't always work that way. This is my ceremony for you, nikâwîs. Let me pour sorrow as I would water onto grandfather rock, let me sweat out possession from every pore I can open, and let that sweet, light smoke of grandmother's hair smoulder into our spirit-bodies. How can I muster us into a prayer, nikâwîs?

If my heart aches, and is in need, then let me say kwêtamâw, which means "s/he is in need, lack, s/he is short in necessities, s/he is without." Let me make for you a parting gift, a maskih-kîwiwat acimowin. Let me play with language, make you something from the rubble of Cree that was stolen from you and me. kwêtamâw nikâwîs, kwêtamâw, or need, morphing into kwêtipinâw, an animate verb meaning "invert, you turn it over." Is this a lesson you teach me as I sit here in my fleeting grief? You, nikâwîs, whom we turned over so many times in that hospital bed so your thinning back and legs wouldn't turn the purple of pressure, those bedsores that coloured you in. You tell me, "Stasis makes stagnancy, ain't you ever watched those ditches fill up and churn into rot right there on the rez, m'boy? Ain't no one's body above the water." Maybe, then, to need you, I mean I need in such a way as to be turned over, to avoid the damage of that stillness, mourning being an open sore that fails to heal because of a break, pain being a pressure that rushes to the spirit-skin. Just look how many bruises I've collected when you look at me in our shared light. kwêtamâw, nikâwîs, kwêtipinâw ahcâhk niyaw, waskawipayiw miyo-pimâtisiwin. My spirit-body, ahcâhk niyaw, links to atâhk miyaw, your star-body, and look at how we braid together and dance across the universe, nikâwîs. Then again, you'll say, "atâhk sounds like 'attack' in English, you need to burst those blisters, that pus is a ridding of infection, an exorcism too, don't you know?"

sâponikan, I'll say, you mean need as in a needle. You'll nod, having picked every foreign splinter from your skin with those needles in nohkôm's tobacco tin: sâponam, s/he goes through it, pierces through the needle eye. sâponam niyaw, you'll nod as the sores on ahcâhk niyaw recede. I'll promise not to cry, even if it means I can't see you anymore, and you'll nod, wrap your arms around me like a webbing, invoke sâponiwew, "s/he goes through people," and I'll feel lighter when I wake.

"See," you'll say in my dreamscapes, "ain't always got to be so goddamned precious, m'boy. Ain't nothing last forever, but the spirit, that sure as hell does, y'know? If you need me, you go ahead and need me, but you remember, kwêtamâw is sâponikan is sâponiwew, and ain't I always been there right beside you all? Heck, look, m'boy," you'll say, "we just sun-danced right there across the prairie sky, sun dogs yacking right along behind us. You remember us this way, m'boy, ain't no need to be so sore."

And all I can yet muster in this moment is: nîmi nicihciy, kisatew nikâwîs manitohkân. nêhiyâwewin tells me that we never say goodbye, we only say see you again, later, kihtwâm nikâwîs kisakihitin kakike, my auntie the wolverine.

And so, just where do you think we'll all be going next?

Me, the
Joshua Tree

YOU AND I share a secret place in Calgary, the Inglewood irrigation canal that is a few kilometres from our home. I show you this place one day when we go for a walk, tell you how I would run through the dog park and down along the canal while exercising, often stopping to wade my hands through the cold waters. In turn, you show me a place beyond the canal, where the railroads cut across Bow sîpîy[1].

After the annihilation leading to the death of our relationship has begun, we walk down to the canal after a weekend of

---

[1] river

stewing in depression. It's a beautiful Sunday; pîsim[2] is there above us, massaging our shoulders until they brown. As we stride along a path, I stop and ask, "Do you hear that?" and you say, "It must be from the golf course nearby." I have stopped us because I hear voices, almost from beneath, as if they were in the catacombs of the canal—a whimpering, maybe; an exultation? What are the trees whispering to us in this moment, what of the water, what of the rocks? We continue on this path you have walked many times, a handful of them to escape me after I have hurt you through words weaponized, and you take me to the clearing.

As we continue through the clearing, we come across a jutting of land and openness of water: Bow sîpiy is here, greets us through its steady rocking. Sometimes a wave is a wave. There are duck feathers strewn about, a carcass, and a firepit here on this little outcrop of land that believes it is a cliff. You say, "Someone has been here, caught a duck looks like," and I think, "I'm so happy they used everything."

We sit on the edge smoking cigarettes. You skip rocks across the lake, and I run my hands through the water, sift my fingers through silt. This whole journey reminds me of the film *Stand by Me*, which is one of my favourites; I feel like I am Gordie Lachance, and here you are Chris Chambers. In this vignette I play in my head, I imagine us having started that fire, roasted that duck, slept here in the tall grasses, let sîpiy sing us to sleep.

---

[2] sun

I'll ask, "Do you think I'm weird?" and you'll say, "Definitely, but so what? Everybody's weird." And in that moment my belly will bloom because this is a moment I have craved since I was a child, latched on to the ghost of Lachance; I live through the intimacy I share with characters whose lives I have imagined. We'll talk into the night, that kind of talk that seems important until, as Lachance narrates, you discover girls. Of course, we have discovered girls—but in this moment, we are also just two queer boys discovering one another, and the landscape around us, and how our bodies are now braids separated, culled for the smudging. How easy is intimacy, honesty, truth, when imagined in a dream or when we are apart? How we grind into one another, spark flints for the fire we let die, and feast through the blaze we create now, here, in this moment, as individuals. In this vignette, I hear you say—by which I mean I hear myself say—"I wish that I could go someplace where nobody knows me." We have come here to see a body—which doesn't exist, because this is a vignette; but we have come nonetheless. And so what I offer up is bodies in multiplicity: the river body, the earthen body, a pocket of air, a breast of rock, bicep of branch, me, you, us. We witness death here too, though in a different fashion from the film, more holistic than nihilistic, that continuum where death kisses birth—and is there even a concept such as division?

I come back into myself, having lived a full life in the briefest of moments while that rock skipped across the lake and your forehead pores swelled so much they began to sweat and your index finger, with its scythe-shaped scar, uncurled from the hook you bent it into—you and me, we have our own sense of time.

You smile at me, I giggle back, and we sit side by side. Across the river, a man fly-fishes. We watch him catch a fish and then leave, climbing back up the hill on the other side. There, a cyclist passes by, singing along to a song he intimately knows. sîsîp[3], niska[4], and ayîk[5] come to visit us as we sit together, kneecaps buckling, maybe even aching to hold one another, and pîsim beats time into our backs, which form continents of sweat. kâhkâkiwak[6] land in the middle of sîpiy, which is disturbed by the leg of a railway. There atop the railings they meet, cawing at one another, feathers extended into hands, greetings; they talk with one another, and we listen, smiling. What are these kâhkâkiwak talking about? Boisterously, they chat as if at a reunion or a send-off—and what's the difference anyway? We sit silently, witnessing askiy[7] talk all around us, a pair of ravens saying, "I love you," in a language not our own—yet maybe also one we know intimately? Raven is a sign, I think; these ones are here to demonstrate the ravenous appetite of finality.

Finality is a horrendous word; it eats, you know? It has teeth. I thought and still think of finality a lot, especially during that

---

[3] duck
[4] goose
[5] frog
[6] ravens
[7] the land

final weekend when we decided to sever and then spent every waking moment together healing. Finality—as severity—is a word that I need to erase from my vocabulary. It's too linear, too colonial. We, of course, as Indigenous peoples, know that finality is simply an opening into continuity. But during that weekend I plagued myself with the word, I swallowed it whole and squawked up a stomachful of knots—meaning, there were continuums there too. My body rejects finality as an end-stop; my own cells fight against this invasion.

It's funny, though, how mourning changes language, the grammar of being. Finality transforms morphologies into a series of becomings and grievings—but in that becoming I find how language wraps around wounds like a suture, and I am a compressor pounding meaning into broken chains. The first time I heard you call me Joshua in the aftermath, my dorsal was spliced in half and I was kinêpik[8] again, tonguing the decadence of a splitting letter: it was like watching how an *A* halves into a broken ladder, and suddenly I was trapped in the abyss of signs. Then I too worked up the effort to transform language: I called you by your name, or friend, and as much as it wounded me to do so, this act told me that transformation always begins with the tongue, that wonderful glossia. When I reminisce about you, I laugh, throwing my tongue into the air as if it were a newborn—and I find a hinterland of thrush growing there upon it. The biosphere, askîy, finds me here too, grows

---

[8] snake

upon my buds: I taste snakeroot, rainwater, chokecherries, the taste of growth is nêhiyâwewin. This thrush, bush, forest-tongue, divides into treaties, a treatise with no subject, and my mouth becomes a geography of grammar. Nothing will ever be the same again, I think. Normal will have to be redefined; grammar, that slick tool, that scaffold, will have to die and lilt into a new language.

IN WHAT WAYS is a manuscript an exhibit? In what ways are these words animate? Maybe you understand these pages as an artifact, sacred words from an NDN; or maybe you read me as a sex worker of language, one who strips and fucks the page and spills himself all over it? Do you clone me? Do you seed me? Do you let narrative germinate? Do you shake the page and expect me to fall out? How do you read me? How do you envision me? Maybe I say I am a broken web, blown into singularity from a wind that knows no bounds? Maybe I say I am sand in an hourglass and you are peeking into granularity? What I will tell you is that this specific chain of letters, spaces, commas, punctuation marks, and white space is in fact an animate being. Through it, you survey my body, my memory, my spirits, my heart, my emotions. You, in this moment, own me, or think you do, even as I escape through the loophole of an end-stop, that damning boulder, that prick of ink that bleeds the skin.

NOW YOU AND I are in Nanaimo, BC, and I am visiting your temporary home. We are in a "sketchy" part of town, as you call it, but it feels familiar—as if poverty has a universal look across Turtle Island: the same siding, the same windows looking like eyes, colours, doors, roofing. Your bed is on the floor, your living room is beautifully nostalgic for the prairies, your patio is littered with cigarettes but well cared for. I crossed on a ferry just to meet you here, dolphins and orca greeting this lonely NDN far from his homeland. The wind salts my face, my pores clog, and I shine in the daylight as my hair tries to free itself from its braids.

I shower while you're at work. Waiting for you to come back to this place you call home, I inspect the inventory of your identities. Smell is such a powerful tool of memory—I pick up your soap and huff before I use it. There are little whiskers attached to it, curlicues; even your body hair spells out stories to me. I bask in the scent of your armpits, your jawline, the way the delicate skin on the bridge of your nose has spread its oils here. I lather myself with your shampoo, heavily so, and I scrub the scalp clean of its dandruff. I rinse myself, dry my hair, and smell the scent of the towel afterwards. I linger like a ghost in the reeds of the fabric, taking it all in, because this is the first time I've seen you in the months since your move and I am a nostalgic person.

When you get home, you offer to show me around the town. We visit the docks, stroll through the downtown, sand and salt water pecking our faces. You take me through a path in Bowen Park, show me the totem poles that have fallen down and are returning to the foliage of their mother's skin. Here: bear, frog, orca, eagle lie side by side, not in a tomb or a finality, but as elders turned newborn waiting to be birthed again into the soil from the roots of saplings turning into children once again. Later we decide to eat dinner, and you take me to the Oxy, a lovely little pub that turns into a karaoke bar later in the evening. We sit in the corner, order a pint each, and sip, massaging the link that is between us, lovers reunited over long distances. A cavalcade of older women jaunt in. One has recently undergone a divorce, and she asks us if we're together. When we muster up the courage to say yes, she eyes us more closely: we might be queers who can navigate her through her breakup. Later, someone sings "Love Shack," and suddenly the whole bar is up and dancing. You and I join the crowd of shimmying folks, across from one another, smiles wide as bucket handles. Your hair bounces when you hop, your hair again a curlicue with those beautiful curls that look like tendrils or foliage, and I am the NDN artifact, a totem pole, melding into them, rotting into nutrient. When the song ends, you go up to speak to the DJ while I sit with another round of beer for us. Then I see you standing alone in the middle of the dance floor, your eyes attached to mine. A song comes on: the twang of country and the familiar banjo of Dolly Parton. You sing "Joshua" to me, and I imagine myself as the isolated, mean, vicious man living alone in a shack with a black dog, while you, as the bouncy-haired Dolly, arrive just in time to find me pondering pandemonium.

I have come here just to meet you.

··

IN A LETTER you send me as we are in the middle of breaking up, you tell me that you "can't see the forest for the trees." In the moment of reading this, my mind becomes a viscous, flattened membrane, pulled to every corner, a stretched deer hide, pounded brain and all. Have I concealed the wilds of this act we call relations? Am I more blockade than blessing? How have you only noticed me, the Joshua Tree, when we are in this hinterland of an ecosystem? As a Joshua Tree, am I not a marker instead of malice? Here, existing as a dagger in the desert of a relationship withered into dust and stone, I see myself: my namesake, Joshua, the waver, the guide, arms upraised in a fashion that promises entrance to a land forgotten—but maybe it is me who has forgotten the system of roots that flourish into growth in a dead home, a dying landscape? I grow in groves fashioned from graves. I think of the Mojave, and I am a kernel of maize that combusts between the pressure of two molars— I need moisture, warmth, I need apocalyptic conditions to blossom into edibility, and I am looking for my sisters, already thrown into a pot of soup. Look at the tree of me and tell me there isn't already a forest grasping for oxygen within me.

Even my bed feels like a canyon these days, my house a desert of a space. The nail holes you leave behind are screeching at me, and all I see are the bones of this home, memory leaking from the punctures, my walls quivering while we are both healing. I run my fingers over the wounds of our home, cartilage snapping. I find studs in the walls by seeking out nail heads and hang pictures over the scarring. The watercolours of a painted bear bleed into the bruised wall and all I have to offer as tincture is the sticky smoke of sweetgrass. I feel sorry for the holes. I see myself in them; I too am spilling memories from a broken abalone while trying to hold the balance of the tide and the weight of this contraption I call a body. How heavy a burden it is to maintain the structure of a home, the flexibility of a memory, the rigidity of a body.

There are days when I wake up expecting to see you across the chasm of my bed. Instead, I find the trace of you, ghost of sweat, the yellow outline of your thigh curled into itself, and I melt into the mattress coils and search in those metal rings for your voice, a cough, the rhythm of your exhumation. I smoke a cigarette on my patio, reel myself in. My neighbour, the tiny mouse I let live in my barbecue, scrambles beneath my feet. I suspect he has become used to sweetgrass embers and the burnt ends of sage I lay in a little bush out back. The grass has been recently cut and there are severed tubes of plants splayed in front of me; I turn my eyes away because I have endured enough massacres in my lifetime. I'm sorry I let the weeds eat away at us, but are weeds not also medicine? I make dandelion tea and I drink the root of you, sunshine and mud and sweat in a teacup.

You will be coming to our old home soon and I will be a red-eyed mess. You'll tell me that I smell of medicine when you hug me, and it is true that I am bathing in the smell of cedar, sweetgrass, and sage. I let the perfume of medicine become a telltale sign of my mourning in these end days of our relationship, even as I am sorry it causes you anxiety. But I need to open the gate to my ancestors. This braid of grass was plucked from the hands of nêhiyaw iskwêw[9] in Mohkinstsis, this sage was a gift from Montana, this cedar from nohkôm in Manitoba: the scent of me, awa maskihkîwiwat,[10] is an expansive geography. Grammar slowly returns to me in the frozen second of its embrace. I laugh because I have no other means of replicating the feeling of breaking.

I TALK OF YOU, of us, to my counsellor in Calgary. She tells me that I need to "tame my illusions." In that moment I catalogue her phrasing—because I think it's beautiful, and also because it expresses a truth I consistently avoid. I have mastered being an illusionist, I am a Mesmer of a man. But I tell no one of this magic I house; instead, I throw up a shimmering veneer and cloak my mind in holograms.

Now, when I think about the ethics of writing non-fiction, I reach back to that moment and this woman counselling me into good health, miyopimatisowin[11]; I see myself sitting there swallowing whole her words like hard bread. What is non-fiction? How is it creative? Why do I add the *C* before the *NF*? Do I do it in order to hide? To vanish into the page so as to disguise the body of truth from you? How do I write respectfully and honestly if I am constantly seeking material out in the

---

[9] Cree women

[10] this medicine bag

[11] nêhiyaw world view of living the "good life" (as in, a good way of being with one's self, one's relations, and the land's self)

world and in the constellations of relations I hold near and dear to my heart, all in order to excavate them so as to narrate this to you? Perhaps I have been bad kin to you and to others— how I devour, never satiated; how I archive you into notations and am never fully listening. This is not something I do in other genres of writing. I conclude that it's a defence mechanism. I become a house of mirrors, let others see me as they wish to and, more importantly, see themselves as beautifully moulded reflections.

When you and I break up, we have a long conversation into the infant hours of the morning. We laugh and share and cry in equal measure, and it feels good, because we have been avoiding these acts of vulnerability for so long. I ask you, "When did you fall out of love with me?" and you, sparked by our stoking an honest fire, tell me, "Eight months ago." This comment shatters me, quaking down the glassware of my illusions, and my stomach becomes a dead star, an exhausted mouth, nefariously nebulous. I feel betrayed, almost used, and I blame myself for weeks afterwards, trying to find a medicinal root in the ecosystem of this pain. I am angry, but I don't know at whom—maybe myself, for having believed in a mirage for months, watering bedrock rather than the fungi I thought could feed us the protein we so desperately needed.

DO YOU REMEMBER our road trip last summer? How we rode across the badlands looking for medicine in the hoodoos? My Blackfoot friends tell me that the hoodoos are sacred, that they are filled with spirits, something I so wholeheartedly believe that I will not camp among them. You and I make the journey over a weekend, singing songs and sharing light as we drive. We stop at Head-Smashed-In Provincial Park along the way, pick sage from the bushes in the parking lot; I still have those bundles in my maskihkiywat[12] at home. There, we see apisimôsos[13] standing on the drop, tongues wrapped around bundles of grass and seeds, and we simply witness them in their glory, reminded that life abounds even in spaces crafted for death. Marmots lounge, bathing in the sun, fattening and resting in nooks, splayed across concrete slabs. You know this world intimately and take the time to teach a visiting family about a particular type of bird. I stare at you in awe and wonder, my mind cascading with the stories that pour forth from your mouth. I bathe in your language; I dry myself off in the shelter of your sunburnt lashes.

We learn of Napi here, the Old Man, who comes running from the west as warm wind, forever chasing another Old Man who runs from the north shooting arrows and bringing winter. We learn about Napi making the earth and moulding people out of mud. "You must be people," he says, making first a woman and a child. I'm reminded of my own creation story, of muskrat diving to the bottom of the ocean to grab a mound of earth and place it on the turtle's back. I'm reminded of you saying once

---

[12] medicine bag
[13] deer

that you felt you had the ocean in you. I think about those churning currents you house and sometimes let crash against your intestines, body full of memory, water laced with trauma. I hope you learn to let the waves settle into the pit of your belly, make a well of an offering. I think, "M'boy, I have the earth in me—and don't we make a beautiful creation story?" In my mind, I sometimes place us into another vignette: me, reaching down into the whole, that cavernous hole, where askîy exists in you, that rich clay. I take a handful, just enough so as not to waste, and I swim back up to the surface of your oceans. There, I take this hand of clay and smear it into the earth of me, that withering garden full of bare root, dry root, starving root, and let the flora of me feast on the most intimate soil of you—we bloom again and I am holy, slathered in silt.

Do you remember us stopping at the little diner, Igloo Café, in Fort Macleod? Our tummies rumble and you pull over at a place to snack—or so we think. I order a two-piece chicken dinner and you a hamburger. When the food arrives, I am presented with two of the largest pieces of fried chicken I have ever seen, an entire cooked chicken atop a bed of french fries. "A snack?" you say. "That's a damn buffet." And we burst into laughter, there in the summer sun of southern Alberta. Later, we ponder ordering ice cream, but I decide against it. We both know what happens when a Cree ingests dairy, and neither of us are prepared for the flatulence that will follow us into the car, into the night, into our blankets, my stomach a playground of foreign milk.

Halfway through our road trip, we stop in Lethbridge, where we decide I'll go in to rent a room with a single queen bed and you'll wait outside so we could both sneak upstairs without having to out ourselves in this little prairie town. We lounge on the bed and I take pictures, both of us giggling like children on this rickety mattress in this colonized town in this broken constellation of a country. Later, we have dinner downstairs in the hotel bar, order wings and beer, play slots. And, as is our tradition, we go to the casino for the evening, where you discover the Simpsons slot machine. We play into the night.

In the morning, we finish our drive down to Writing-on-Stone Provincial Park. I am afraid of rattlesnakes and you assure me that you'll keep watch for them. We meander through hoodoos in the dry bone heat of the badlands, find thicket, listen to the love songs of birds, and emerge into the playground of stone whittled into hoodoos. The whole of Milk River is there, rushing excitedly. You tell me stories of your family, of your grandfather's relationship to this river, of its connection with Saskatchewan, with your hometown, the Cypress Hills, the monarchs—you're a teacher to me here, and I am studious inside your joyfulness. We sit in a hoodoo and ponder the dreams of stone, will ourselves to name this home as it ought to be: Áísínai'pi. Listen for the manitowâk[14] who place story in our nail beds. This is a place of interconnection, where the physical and the spirit worlds kiss; we are in the cavity of these

---

[14] spirits (animate)

worlds, colliding with one another, and I wait for them to wink at me, tell me to rinse off the soup of pupa in the waters. We hike to see "The Battle Scene," a petroglyph etched into the side of Áísínai'pi's cliff, a breast of earth. Here I see myself defeated as a nêhiyâw, but I don't shy away from this shame; I thank it in this Blackfoot world where I am a guest. We survey the etchings of the battle, "Retreat Up the Hill of 1866," and I look down at my forearm, at the fossa of my elbow, tricep, armpit, and find myself a pictograph: you are carved into the walls of me and I find joy in knowing I house you too.

As we drive away from this place, we listen to Loretta Lynn's "High on a Mountain Top." She giddies into lyric— "God fearin' people simple and real"—and we see Chief Mountain steadfast in the distance, Nínaiistáko, and avert our eyes so as not to stare too long. okîmaw wâciy, hill of sweetgrass, overseer of Niitsitapi, place maker of divinity, we hide our eyes so as not to bring forth the end of day, or even days, that this hill foretells. We are weary during this drive home, hair burned, skin pink, stomachs barren wells. You nap, and as we pass Oldman River, I whisper, "See, Napi has come to wave goodbye." I thank the trout, the prairie, the sheen of rainbow scales swimming into aperture, and the gracefulness of a creator not my own. Open me to aperture, nitôtem[15], the w/hole through which light travels, because I am full of terror.

..

---

[15] my friend

YOU GIFTED ME so much in the few short years we spent together, nitôtem, kinânâskomitin.[16] There's something profound about time for a queer person and an Indigenous person; I think of how many "foundational moments" I missed out on, ones that are so easy for others to have, like graduations, high school romances, slow dancing. Jack Halberstam writes about the registers of queer time, and in this moment, when I am alone, without companion, I am nervous of men again—because you built for me an oasis where my body, in its broken states, its withered states, its atrophied states, could be a blessing. In this register of time outside the oasis, I am learning to be comfortable with my body again.

Here, while I write this, I find you everywhere in my small hometown of Selkirk, Manitoba: there you are eating steak in Barney Gargles, here you are keeping me warm in my childhood bedroom, and over here you are still sitting with me around our firepit. I'm remembering too much, too quickly, this river throws me beneath its current. As I write, it is raining, and I think: even the sky is crying, kîsîk has come to say kihtwâm.

The greatest gift you ever gave me was to attend nîtisân's[17] wedding. Do you recall?

I am my sister's maid of honour, and I am nervous, sweating in the dry August heat. I look over to you sitting by nikâwiy,

---

[16] my friend, thank you

[17] my sister's

nohtâwiy, ekwa nohkôm,[18] and you throw me that shy smile—
and suddenly I feel prepared to steer this event. You are a
beauty of a man, sitting there in your baby-blue suit jacket,
white shirt, black tie, your facial hair a bonnet around your
face. I think: However did kitchi manito[19] ever think me
worthy of such a gift?

At the reception afterwards, I help the wedding party clean
up, and when I finish, I come out to the dance floor and find
you there with my younger cousins. These are shy rez girls who
shiver in the city, and you bring out their confidence, their
joy—you enchant it out from within them and let them spill
smiles across the room. I marvel at your ability to do that for
people, to find your way through the copse of people's pain in
order to dive into their happiness. We all dance to country
songs, and you two-step with my mother, and I am full of glee
to see how my family wraps around you, lets you in, embraces
you as kin. I go up to the DJ, request "Your Song" by Elton
John, and stand across the floor from you. As the piano keys
tinkle, Elton's voice comes on. Throughout my life I have listened to this song repeatedly, imagining me and another dancing to it, slow, breath tempered and hot, until at the end we kiss,
unabashed, nerved, steadfast against any eyes that may look on
with desire, envy, or hatred. You hear the music and look over
at me, and I walk towards you. We grab hands and interlock,

---

[18] my mother, my father, and my grandmother
[19] the Creator

dancing at that wedding—and I am in tears. I have longed for this gentle embrace all my life. We sway in circles on a cleared dance floor, nearly everyone in my family watching us, because they know this is my song, and you kiss me after it is done, and we hold each other for a few seconds that feel like eternity to me—and now, when I miss you, I remember us this way, two prairie queers celebrating the generosity of an accepting land and a blanket of a family.

No man has ever given me the cornucopia of maskihkîy[20] that you have, m'boy. In that moment, time collapsed and churned into a new world: queer time intersecting with NDN time. This fusion birthed a seedling of a world that I attach to my belly button and nurture continually—and my body aligns, however briefly, as a man who belongs to his true age. You have transformed my worlds for me, and I am no longer a changeling.

I HAVE LAMINATED you into the photo album of wahkohtowin I call my life, and you're imprinted there. There are moments I highlight, such as the photograph I have of you and nohtâwiy on either side of me, all three of us hugging tightly in the dusk of St. Andrews. I have craved this wholehearted acceptance for so long, and you brought it about; you, who love my family so much, teach me what it means to truly respect a person. Or the photo of us in a hotel in downtown Vancouver: I am wearing

---

[20] medicine

red plaid and smiling, braces and all, still practising how to hide my teeth, and you are in a white button-up shirt with abstract blue faces painted on it. We are hugging in the bathroom, taking a selfie, smiles so big our gums are showing. You tell me not to be ashamed of my mouth. We walk down Davie Street, through Gastown, holding hands, and never once do we care who witnesses this. We make "blanket forts" in our hotel room later, regress into boyhood, naked, cuddling, making love, admiring the vastness of one another. And there is a photograph of us walking across the Cambie Street bridge in that same city, our hands around one another's hips. The sun is setting, a tint of blue stains the camera lens, but we know what we are looking at: pîsim is there, kissing our faces like atîm, saliva and sweetness and dog licks and all.

I THINK ABOUT the word "ex"—another word I want to remove from my lexicon because it is a signifier I cannot attribute to you, nitôtem. What a disgusting word, with its colonial sentiment of ownership, its finality; and what a heterosexual word. The word "ex" performs what it says: it cuts, disfigures, it snaps meaning off history. Instead, we will define ourselves for ourselves.

During our breakup, we live together for nearly three weeks. I refuse to let you sleep on a friend's couch out of care for your tender back. In this time, we revel in one another's joy, share stories we've never shared, released from the weight of the encompassing robe we call a relationship. Unfettered, we are free to be ourselves, to see one another in new light, to share vulnerabilities and traumas without fear of triggering or offending the other. This is something we have not had in many months, this fluidity of being. Why are we so afraid to criticize one another? Why do we shy away from pain? I tell you that criticism can be a generosity, a medicine even, and critique can be a salve that sharpens joints and repairs tears. I know this now, and I return to my teachings, return to honesty; that is the only gift I have yet to give you. And I ask: Will you humble me, m'boy?

Why do so many of my kin and relations tell me to excise you from my life, to move on, to let go? Why do we, collectively, hold on to this idea that we must release the gifts we are given by others? Of course, I can see why many people would want to exorcise past lovers from their life, especially if they have experienced domestic abuse, rape, or emotional degradation, but ours was and is a relationship of transformation. I loathe that word "ex" for you; I refuse to call you that. You tell me that what's left is the strongest thing we've ever shared, that the skeleton of our friendship has gotten us through to this point in our lives, makes all of this pain worth it. My counsellor tells me to think of our breakup less as a "letting go" and more as a "moving through": we can carry one another like beaded medallions we fashion with pride, and dance with into the day, both bound to hide through the giving of a needle's eye.

· ·

WHEN YOU BROUGHT your keyboard into our once-home, it was so large it had to have its own room—our second bedroom. You, a musician of a man, I ask if you'll play me a song. I realize that this is the first time I have ever asked this of you, and I am full of regret. You are wearing a colourful scarf to hold back your hair, and the sweater I sometimes like to steal and wear for comfort. You sit down on the piano stool and I tell you to wait, I want to record this moment. You ready yourself. I lean against a bookshelf and you unleash orality. The keys ring out with a beautiful melody and you begin to sing Alison Krauss's cover of "Till I Gain Control Again," a song you tell me you listened to repeatedly during your decision process about our relationship. I'm brought back to a moment when I was watching you on our couch. You were lounging there wearily after a day of teaching at a nearby Hutterite colony; the blinds on the window were open and bars of light dangled across your body, dust in the sun dancing across your skin and hair. In this vignette, I moved towards you, hugged you, placed your arms around my neck, cupped your legs into the crooks of my arms, and lifted you up—and you gazed up at me, lips pouted to kiss, and instead I blew into your hair, let fly the seed pods caught there, and flowered my house into a terrarium. When I return to the present, you are mid-song and I am weeping willow, face soaked in tears. Yet I am happy in this moment that you have gifted me. I intend to hold you to your word that you'll "come home again" in some limited, tangential capacity; and I promise to stand brightly, holding you, until we become daisies of men.

..

WE WALK TOGETHER and you teach me how you see the land. Starlings murmur to the soft thrum of the Bow's ripples. You teach me about them, about how they're an introduced species, a colonizing bird. They sing whirring songs high in the trees— birds of mimicry. I imagine them re-enacting this moment we are sharing: one of us in grief, the other a doppelgänger. Later, they become a haunting presence, endlessly remixing songs of mourning, saying your name when I walk this path alone. I imagine they mock me in a Shakespearean fashion, song rushing from their gizzards, confusing me to the point where I believe I am being asked for more time, and I panic, a prisoner to my fictional vignettes, unable to differentiate between what is health and what is ruin, my heart aflutter with a murmuration. Why did you steal the egg, starling? Why crack open the shell to fling out a growing wing? What are you trying to teach me in this moment?

When I return to myself, you are beside me, the scent of wolf willow wafting around you, a sweet musk.

You stop, kneel down, beckon me to look. Yellow flowers blossom in a patch of sunlight: buffalo beans. You tell me a story about this plant, how a girl in your hometown ate the toxic pea and had to get her stomach pumped. It's a gorgeous plant, but vicious in its delights. This is a plant you know intimately; it calls you home, and in this moment, as your story anchors you temporally and geographically, you are healing. I lean in to witness the majesty of this. I think of telling you that buffalo beans are also waypoints, indicators of rich game, of bison being ready for the hunt. But I pause to see the prairie in you, your blue eyes alight. You are living sky, and in this moment I take the time to immerse myself in the pool of your iris.

We continue along the path, looking for the refuge of a particular spot we like to visit. A new bridge has been built to cross a little stream, a bridge constructed from a pallet. You say to walk quickly over it so as to maintain the weight on the board; if I wobble, or stumble, or stop completely, gravity will crack me in half. I listen, thinking more about the foundation of me than the unsteady piece of wood underfoot. On the other side, the sun looms over us; pîsim lets us know that they will sit with us, guiding. We are in the shadow of a power line, a menacing giant, whose rickety metal bones cast bars across the grass. We are trapped within its shadow—and we both stop to look up, shield our eyes from the sun, observe the power line in its talltale rapture. Everything seeks to overpower us, engorge us, to take away this journey we call an afternoon stroll. We stare down the tower, two Davids eyeing behemoth, and conquer this looming presence before continuing on. We walk to the clearing in silence, save for the medicine song of a consistent wind.

We sit along the edge of the Bow, feet dangling in the cool water, and I light a cigarette. Staring solemnly, stoically, at the contours of the river, our knuckles brush, bones aching to touch. You skip rocks across the body of the water, and I slice open a cigarette to say a prayer to sipîy. A kin of mine told me to pray for water when smudging, and I practise this when I light my medicines. He says he doesn't yet fully understand this ritual, but it means something different to everyone, and that's the point: we all have differing relations to bodies of water and the water in our own bodies. I think, "What better way to pray for water and healing than to go to the body itself?" I wave my hands in the tide and in nêhiyâwewin I ask sipîy to cleanse you and me both, to soothe the friction burn of peeling our braid apart, and to think of us in a sun shower.

When I'm finished, I see that you are watching me. I call you over, and together we let the tobacco offering be swallowed by sipîy. You tell me that Bow sipîy goes into the Saskatchewan River, which divides into the North and South Saskatchewan Rivers and ultimately empties into the Lake Winnipeg watershed before exiting the continent at Hudson Bay. You tell me this for perspective: "When you put down your tobacco in the Bow, you send medicine home to Manitoba." I will never forget this lesson. I am praying for the good home, a refuge where I can store that which is us.

We sit side by side, both knowing what is to come next—although one can never properly prepare for doom. I ponder this evolving inquiry: In what ways does a relationship call for a division of the self? Is it cellular division? What kind of dismantling does a relationship require—or perhaps rather than dismantling I mean augmentation, that something must be lost or forgone in order to fill in the nuclei. I rub your back, feel the tips of your vertebrae, this broken part of you I ache to care for. When I think of your spine, and the dreadful accident that happened just moments into our relationship, I nearly drown myself in empathy. M'boy with the broken back that will whittle into a bear trap over time. Did you know the word for backbone or spine in nêhiyâwewin is mâwikan? I break the word down into its elements, search for covalence, find the following: mâwiso, to pick berries; mâwihkas, to cry after him; mâwimowin, crying for help or a cry of pain. Can I offer you solace, medicinal story? Will you let me craft a basket for you, brimming with the sage I save for you? M'boy with the pîkopayiw mâwikan,[21] I eat from the bowl of your vertebrae, give offerings in their convex. I pick berries, in full-iskwêw fashion, for you to feast on. I lay otêhimin pahkitinikana[22] in the discs between your columns, plants I've plucked with my teeth, held in the mouth, seeds I store beneath the tongue, kin I've laid down tobacco for. In those moments when you cry for help, body brimming with pain, mâwihkas, I offer wihkaskwa, braids of sweetgrass, which I weave in between the structure of you from cervical to lumbar. In exchange for namâwîyak, I eat the word, chew it into cud, regurgitate victory from violence, and spit out mâmawi, or "together, in full number, as a group"— I find you again, mâmawi-tahto, nîcimos. Even in these planes of pain, I find relations and I seek to transform them for you. It is my right as an elder in the making; I owe you reciprocity.

Knowing what is to come, I offer you this word: ka pîkopayik wihkihtowin, a breakup. See how these words

---

[21] broken back
[22] strawberry (heart berry) seeds

revolve in continuums? M'boy with the pîkopayiw mâwikan, we are stretching nêhiyâwewin to fit around us for this impending decision, sheathing ourselves in language; we become pîkopayiw, broken; but look, m'boy, look at how linguistics hold us, animate us. As I do with your back, I do with our relations: I crunch language into new meaning, find signs in the gravel of my breaking molars, transform ka pîkopayik wihkihtowin into kaskamocâyâwin wahkohtowin—or, "we build up inertia in an enclosure to enact 'all my relations.'" Let's do this together, nicîmos kwêskinaw nitôtem, wichihin nanâtawihiwêw ekwa niya asotamowin koci nâtamâkêwin kiya wakinew kîkway ka pihtokepayik miyomahcihowin, nitasotam mâmawi kimîyosinaw.[23]

You rest your head on my shoulder and I wrap my arm around you, squeeze the softness of your torso, huff in your now-wolfen scent—it is almost metallic, that pleasant smell of sodium and wet zinc. I think again about finality and choke myself. But you say you love me, and the hold breaks. I tell you that I have never loved so wildly as I have and do for you. And then you look up at me, the sun drowning in the well of your eyes. I wish I knew how to slow down time, to enjoy, cherish, revel in the acts of love we gifted one another. I tell you I don't remember our last good kiss, and I cry thinking that our final

---

[23] My lover turned/changed into my friend, help me heal and I promise to try to help/support you to bend into good health/good feelings/the act of feeling euphoric; I promise, together, we are good (as two people).

love act was a simple peck goodbye. I ask: "Can we have one last good kiss before we end this?" And you nod, say, "Of course." You kiss me and I grab the coattails of time to archive this. Everything pours into and out of this act we share—so much that, if I were to narrate it here, I would fail before I begin. We hold the kiss as a man fishes across the river, cyclists pass by, a train conductor wails steam into the air. Beaver, loon, duck, starling, wolf willow, buffalo bean, grass, river, rock, feather all come to witness this moment of goodbye, and I hold the kiss steady. We have never been much for public affection—when you grab my hand in a movie theatre, scared by a horror film, I sometimes flinch—and the optics of queerness often terrify me in spaces safe or otherwise. But I hold you here, lips pursed, and I am packing in as much as I can fit, willing myself into becoming stone, or a fossil, or an arrowhead, or petrified wood for you to take with you. I wish I could have gifted you more moments like this during our time together. There is still so much I want to show you—and I will, but as I said, finality is obsessed with punctuation. When we pull apart, I lick my lips and savour the rue of your saliva, a distinct flavour: smoke, peaberry, zephyr. We sit in this peaceful sliver we have created, together, holding tightly on to one another, and now I am a man simply full.

In this stasis I call wreckage, I thank you for releasing me from the throes of what we'd called a flow. And while we walk back to our temporary home, I murmur my name to a starling so that it'll follow you, guide you, and you won't lose

me in the mourning. I prayed to Creator every day during
these difficult times: I smudged until my lungs blossomed
maskosîy[24] seeds; I danced across the sky, flew to mother in a
dream, drank the rich, musty water of sîpiy, baptized myself
with amisk[25] in her dam; I shared kinosêw[26] bones with
wacask[27], ripped the wing off a damselfly and glued it on my
back; I split open the abdomen of a kwêkwêkocîs[28] and drank
its luciferin; I chewed the sinew of maskwa[29]. I did all this to
pray and say, Please, Creator, don't let the world take this love
away, and what I found in the remains of this sweaty, bloody
mess was that sâkihitin had shape-shifted, planted itself into
a new body—and now we are hooved and galloping in the
afterglow of a morning transformed.

In that glow I exist, me, the Joshua Tree, guiding you to the
good home that exists both within and without me—and I
hope you'll take me, at least as a seedling, into the gardens of
your mitêh mîkiwâm.[30] I revel in your joy, m'boy. And I carry
you with me, lovesap moulded into the crevice of this splitting
heartwood.

---

[24] grass

[25] beaver

[26] fish

[27] muskrat

[28] firefly

[29] bear

[30] heart home

The Pain
Eater

I HAVE RETURNED to the mountains, squeezed between the breasts of Radium's cliffs again. I have returned to the navel of thought from which I spewed forth the final breaths and commas of *Jonny Appleseed*, nesting in the Rocky Mountains. Staring out at the lone edge of a raised hillside, its convex aperture—it, too, pretending to be a mountain in the making, willing the wind to propel it into a taller vista, wanting to wave to the snowcaps reflecting pîsim into the needles of elder pine—I splice open a cigarette to lay down tobacco for guidance and reciprocity from my ancestors, here in a territory far from my own. I take off my moccasins and socks, dig my toes into the mud, curl into consonant, and arch my feet up into the sun rising above the mountaintops. I close my eyes. Here my sole too becomes a bowl, and I foreground the arch of my foot against the bevel of the Rockies. We craft a parallax of containers thirsting to be filled, one of earth, one of snow; one of ground, one of sky—creation in the making. Fill me, I say to no one visible, although everyone I have ever touched and loved stands here on the hill, in the dogged light of near morning, raising their naked feet into a sky rising too. We pull the hill up with us, granting its wish, becoming a mountain, becoming elder, becoming unmoored from the sewage pipes you hide, my hill, and enter anew into definitions with no score or merit in this bull's eye we call "English." And there begins a horizon from which I gallop into language, the swath of kin I house—now upside down, by which I mean right side up, feet planted into Sky World, their long braids and fingers saplings and witness-trees reaching for me, tickling me with foliage, brushing my hair that is knotted into a nest from the violent whippings of merely surviving.

I tell myself this richness of being, singular yet wholly connected, is a breadth of breath that expands beyond the monotony of being I've so carefully contained myself within. And yet the refrain that is housed within me now, in this particular moment we find ourselves in globally—"Please stop, you're killing me"—rings continually, like a chime in a windstorm.

When I return into myself, I remember why I have come here. My aunties are selling raffle tickets on Facebook for two children's bicycles to raise enough money for a headstone for my uncle, who passed away handfuls of years ago. Another aunt of mine I picture clutching my uncle's ashes, contained in a soup pot, waiting for the moment we can all meet again and properly release him back into the breathing roots, the lungs of his trapline—Patsy Cline and Garth Brooks harmonizing in her home on vinyl loops as she mourns. I think of my grandmother, Rose, who yet sits unmarked in Saskatoon, her burial rites and recognition a poem in the landscape of Literature— the poem, like her autopsied body, taken apart and examined by doctor and scholar alike. This ritualistic asking, this giving of medicine, then serves as both gratitude and an overloaded act of grieving.

I walk back to the cabin I have come to write in, the Highwomen's "Cocktail and a Song" playing in my AirPods. Amanda Shires warbles: "Don't you look at me, girl, like I'm already gone / the day is close, it won't be long." All of this, I wonder, for whom? Or for what? I think of nohtawiy, of nikawiy, of wahkohtowin; I think of the conversations I've had with many of the "you's" in this manuscript, having drafted contingency plans for the "what if," should the moment we contract the sickness of pandemic take us too soon. I think of the half-joking, half-dead-serious inquiries about what would become of this manuscript if I were to wilt into a flattened petal, a dried bouquet of wildflowers, alone in a bed, tubed and plastic-lunged in a hospital cot, if I were lucky, or caked over alone in a bathroom, peeling oxygen out of the tiled floorboards.

How close is the day if I close the day prematurely in this gratuitous grieving? I want to ask Brandi Carlile if she ever became a crowned sparrow, and if so, could she teach me how, too? I want to ask if she ever unstrapped herself from that wheel in Laredo. I am trying to do the same, Creator knows, so let me roll this back for you.

It's nearing Christmas in 2020 and I am driving home from Alberta to Manitoba at a frenzied speed of 130 kph. The prairies are easy, you can always spot a cop from miles away in the flatlands, their cruisers a white stain on this earthen mound—the Trans-Canada Highway a gauze to the spilling I am conducting. I wrap the Cypress Hills windings around me, a simple tourniquet: concrete, rose bush, sagebrush. I am racing home to save myself. Bits of me flake off like petrified bark in the gusts of Saskatchewan winds that pour into my car as I open the window. I watch the skin on my arm blow away into dust in this squall, dance upon my dash, squeeze itself out of the tiny crack of my window, and mushroom into living sky.

When I cross the Manitoba border, the night is thick, viscous. I meander through its gels, sticky from its humid sweat, ectoplasm, wet from panting, dry, cracking tongue in want for thirst. It's here—after weeks of smudging for communion, not of the Christian style, but with union of community for the sake of surviving a pandemic that requires the obliteration of touch, of intimacy, of a kiss to shotgun breath back into the body—I witness magic. Carlile howls into the sky, glazed with stars that look like sugar and pinhole, "You should always let the sun go down on your anger / let it burn you to sleep." I see a shooting star dart across the sky—something I have not witnessed in the light pollution of urbanity and fluorescent nettings in a dog's age. I wish upon this star's particles and granularity, upon the trail of life fleeing from its now-foreign head, upon this light pouring into my retina, a dying flare, mercenary. The body disintegrates, but that is not to say it dies; it transforms into mineral, potassium, into oxide and oxygen. We always return to our mother. "When you're home, you're already home," Carlile sings. The luminosity of this majesty overcharges my senses, history now writ as a dying version of me smoking in my truck, lips pouted out of a cracked window, snaking out of aged skins.

In another history, which is to say that present moment in which I experienced this, and this future ledge from which I perch now, the sky blooms like a wound, a corsage, or a wormhole, or a needle's eye, sâponikan, and I thread into its weavings, thrust—I am dancing sky, holding burning cherub, babies rushing into elderhood, weeping for motherhood; and I am birthgiver, star walker, the grandness of a body whose pouch I zippered out of to be here in this body named Joshua. The sky is ablaze—not with apocalypse, although surely this is an ending, but with a mouth slightly ajar, teeth askew, and tongue slicked into a curve to suckle milk and galactic dew. Here, Creator blesses me, a bobbin now unwound fully on the seat of his Chevrolet, and tells me, "Take what you need, take it all, this is a gifting for you—but make sure you gift something back, m'boy." As the night sky becomes an inferno of babes scraping across the belly of some *thing* we might call God, I am presented with wishes aplenty, and I ask for health and happiness for those I love and care for. And as the presentation of floral fires ends, one lone meteor stops, momentarily, and winks at me. Its light fills my mouth like a blooming, a feast of magic, a feast of divinity. I wish then for happiness for myself—in the form of something material, something that can hold me, kiss me; someone upon whose palms I can draw hearts into their broken lines, and whose intersecting histories, wrought upon their calloused skin, I can smooth like wind caressing sandstone. I wish for partnership. I wish for caretaking and excitement. I wish for kinder tomorrows. I wish for joy buttoned into being. "And I am leaving / oh, I am tired / and I'm coming home / 'cause I am yours," Carlile hums into a barrelled echo. I orate all of this to say: in you I smell the rich grains of asteroid and planetary parallaxes; I taste honeydew when I mouth your name into air; and my belly blossoms with seedling and story when I drift into dusk, your richness a buffalo hide, a papoose for cradling into soft sleep. I find the wish granted, in these limited but wide connections we share across latitude and nationhood.

You're a skeleton key found in dust and pixel. I want to wish to thank Creator for putting mud to rattle with a lipsticked kiss to form you into being, so that we could find one another, here, at the end of the world—holding hands as the nation-state burns and we emerge into newer horizons rich with possibility and potential. I speak here of a wish for radical change and rhizomes of care—out of a sense of global care but also, for once, out of selfishness too. I think the world of this pronoun "you"— so here I'll build a world from a pronoun, and balloon it into wishes. I place a kiss into the wind in the hope it finds you when you need love. I whisper to rain and snow a love coo, so that when you're feeling lonely, sweet words will tickle your cochlea. In this limited materiality, across the chasm of kilometres, I want you to know that along the bent line of sundown there is a person waving endlessly, waiting, patiently, even lifetimes if needed, for the moment he can celebrate a ballet of bodies, the warmth of skin touching, the shiver of excitement, the brush of lip skin on lip skin, and the sifting of finger through hair. A wish, one I saved from that Manitoban evening, I send to you in eastward gusts. Take it; I hope it works for you too. My affection pours forth from my body tectonically, a gifting to the "you's" of this manuscript—and I am emptied abalone, shell of ash and smudge.

Now back in my body, meteor shower having ended, that lone winking comet swallowed by the sky, we return to nothing but deadlight and sky-scarring—the severance of our connection to dimensionality now a light line on the skin of infinity. And I, like âtim, put my head out of the window and lap up the remnants of that comet's Sky Peopled wish. Having scraped the sky and killed a bird, I thank the comet for its gifts, untie my shoe, and toss it out the window as a promise of cycles of return.

I am racing home for rejuvenation at the height of isolation, suffering intimacy starvation, having worked vast numbers of hours with little to no reprieve from my own warring thoughts and anxieties, from which I have emerged slightly charged but nearing depletion after an encounter with suicidal ideation. This running home is more than a reunion; it is a raging against the death knell the world has been ringing, both in this particular momentous pandemic but also in the echo of those church bells that have been tolling their death hymns for Indigeneity since 1492.

"Please stop, you're killing me" is my refrain, accompanying this ominous tinkling.

Lately, I've been alarmed by the question "How are you?" It is a bewildering jab, and I swallow pain whole and regurgitate little worlds for others even as I exist in the canyon of a junkyard spelling out nihilism on the jagged rims of tins. How do we care for one another when we're so entirely exhausted on multiple planes of historical and intergenerational existence? How do we hold one another when even the pronoun "you" feels more like a stitch ripper than a darting needle? Even prior to this pandemic, conversations, primarily with BIPOC and queer folks, around mental health and wellness were choreographed dances indeed—but now I find the peppering of "how" alongside the pronoun "you" to be an adverse adverb that hinges on the profane. A simple asking can so easily become a violent undoing. I am teaching myself the ethics of asking and engaging, of when that moment and level of trust is correct, even with the most beloved people in life—teaching myself how to care for ourselves and one another on the brink of obliteration.

. .

ON VALENTINE'S DAY, 2021, my apartment floods from a burst pipe in my living room. I am informed that the rupture was caused by the cold air from an open window—this, after the stifling heat in my apartment had only recently been fixed. I awake that day to two men knocking on my door, one a condo manager, the other a contractor who will temporarily fix the issue.

Both men come into my apartment, and the contractor begins fixing the pipes as the "building manager" surveys my home—looking at the Simone McLeod, Jerry Whitehead, Pat Bruderer, and Kent Monkman paintings on my walls before announcing, "I didn't realize you were so cultural; I think it's great the Natives are still so in touch with their culture." The man continues to inspect my condo, noting the differences in my layout as compared with others in the building. He comes across a bullwhip my father bought me when I was a child. "You shouldn't use the thermostat as a hook for your sex toys," he says. I can only imagine the thoughts running through his head as he sees pictures of queer folk on my fridge, an embroidered "Queer" tapestry, my Eighth Generation Snagging Blanket draped across my couch, and smells the lingering scent of sweetgrass from the previous evening's smudge. I entertain him to busy his wandering eyes, his dirtied, sullied fingers, and to abate the power he holds over me as a tenant in the building.

After finishing with the radiator, they both leave. Hours later—my radiator pulled apart into pieces and lying on the floor, my living room's contents shifted into my tiny kitchen and hallways, the apartment floor's carpet and floorboard ripped up, and the drywall pulled off to dry the insulation—the repair agency installs large, cumbersome, noisy fans in my condo. I ask for an update, knowing I cannot safely live in this place, much less work or house my dog. Chief, my German shepherd pup, is kennelled for three days and I am left to stay in my bedroom, barricaded in from the furniture and artwork scattered around the apartment for the drying process. I sit cross-legged on the floor, a life's worth of collected furnishings and decor displaced around me like a cemetery: a fossilized bison tooth found in Eastend, a painted rock from my niece, my father's engraved Zippo, my great-grandmother's Wades, and the Inuk lance that carved kiyâm into my wrist. Amongst this inventory of rubble, I stare at my walls, this sanctuary I once called grace and refuge. Here, again, my home is scalped of its animations; I sit now in a haunted house I once revived only to let it wither in the cold snap of an Albertan winter. The spirit of the house is splayed and stretched, without an offering, at the hands of yet another settler uncovering the anthropologic without apology. When I wake from this grieving trance, I see the outlines of archived joy traced on the exposed granite flooring in chalk and dust. My home is a microcosm of the nation-state: a stalwart vision of ruination. In this I include, too, my body—the visage of my innerness kneeling on the floor behind a veil of hair, hands splayed into prayer, the buckskin of chest alit with holes: some bullet-shaped, others hitch-scarred.

In the morning I wake and survey the aftermath of this crime scene: the removal of artwork from my walls, inked with oil and greased fingerprints; my carved wooden eagle's beak broken off; ceremonial feathers strewn on the ground; and a beaded earring crushed beneath steeled boot. My condo's upending, its brokenness, mirrors me in this moment as I pack up the home that displaced me. My retreat to a new, more stable place is welcome, but it's the undressing, the undoing, the unlevel of removal from wall and mantel that gives me pain in my chest. The unmitigated destruction of home in the middle of global destruction. The act of packing becomes one of mourning: here I find gifts, love letters, and goodbye notes from the multiples of "you's" addressed in this book. But the real harm I feel is that of violation—the forced entry of and for white folks, the anonymity of touch, broken rostrum and enamel like the snapping of limb and cartilage, the destruction of this place I named sacred. That sacredness is trampled as the world is aflame with ecological shifts and pandemic breath. I feel again as I did when I crashed into this condominium's carpeted floors like Sky Woman, reeling back the bobbies and cogs of my body and dressing the wounds of bruise and rape.

Just when I am settled and feeling safe from this flight into a new home, one of you will ask, "How are you?"—and I will unravel like yarn, drowning out all sound and sight. I will weep the sorrows of these events; I will weep the histories of epidemic and pandemics that I have survived already ancestrally; I will weep the almighty cry that throws everyone within earshot from their bones and blood. The thrush of unmitigated sorrow becomes a saving grace in this moment, for my eye is the only reprieve from gust and blow. I will not be able to answer this question—I will just ask you to hold me. May your arms with their brisk, rough prairie hairs, with their woodlands grit, hold steady a body exploding like an infant star into fractal configurations. pimâtisiwin, I will coo into my linings, kiss into my arms, let me leach from this embrace a bit of joy and futurity— let me live awhile yet.

"Please stop, you're killing me," I'll say as I hold this wreckage like a garbage dump in the contraption I call a body—and I'll will myself to smile, dry enzymes from cheek and collar, and continue into a Zoom meeting, wholly performative of and drunk for this foreign verb we name joy.

I CONTINUALLY FIND myself making plans with kin for when this is "over." While hopeful, this repeated deferral reminds me of how embroiled we are within a system of continual warring. When is over? Will that day ever come? Will our collective hope bloom into revolutionary NDN joy when we emerge on the other side? Can our feet carry us across such hilltops and chasms? What is over, and where is over? In nêhiyâwewin, we say kisipi as a means of signalling an end, a finishing. If over were a place, I would name it homeland—signalling a finale, but also an entrance into possibility, for this world we inhabit is overwrought, overwritten. I would name over a space in which futurities lie, rich, dark tendrils that thirst in the space of overness—over being the potential for Indigenous excellence in this collective grief we call occupation. I would name over the Dover Hills, my river spot in Mohkinstsis; I would name over the feeling of sitting along the Bow River reading Alexander Chee, shirtless, in tiny swim trunks, alone save for pîsim above. Over would be the ease of stripping off one's shirt without the burden of body dysmorphia—how easy, then, to remove and fully be. Over would be the splendour hidden in the mundane, this power so easily taken for granted. Over would be a bingo hall full of NDN kin bucking for their numbers, trolls and lucky charms atop numbers, scrounging change for chip-ins for a Friendship Centre hot dog. Over would be a naming ceremony, would be a revolutionary pow-wow, would be the rolling head of John A. Macdonald later becoming a terrarium in the aftermath of the nation-state, would be the concrete crown of Queen Victoria engrossing the head of an orange-shirted child. kisipi, I return to the end, which is never a finishing but a beginning. I return to the Bow, to the Red, to the Milk—I return to the river to ponder a finale. This river connects us all; we each have our spot, which we some-times share, and which in turn I'd call a truer kind of nudity than the act of undressing. Here we each have a spot to mourn, play, make love, and self-create. kisipi, sipiy, kisipikamâw, môskinew—and I am slathered in holy silt from which I'll spew into you the bile of creating clay.

I strip myself of the preservation of colonial wax, static and immobile, encasement and showcase, hulking statuette frozen in time, in amber. Look at how my Indigeneity shimmers in the daylight, in this form that is a body that never knew embodi-ment, a noun beyond body with no properness, a portmanteau, love child of body and of end. Here verbology will unmoor from its predatory classifications and retire itself into herbology; and there, too, its sheathings will peel florally, and from its predicate will emerge the seedlings of kin, infant in their babbling, saying of this subjecthood: over, over, over. And here this "you" disintegrates between the crushing of prefix and suffix, and all I will know then is the rooting of osihew. Should I say, then, that "over," in its animate beings, kisipayiw, might be this verbnoun atop the Golden Eyries—my ears tilted into the wind to hear the doom cry of finality, because when the end rings its end, the mountains will move again, tired from their cumbersome slumber, tired from being bent into a V from ear to pelvis, and stretch into a thrust. The land, like the body, teaches us the fundamental rule of ending: that no such thing exists, no suffix of "-ed" shall ever touch the prefix of "pre-" and even a body in its most cellular state knows this.

We always begin at the end.

I picture myself spread-eagled atop the Blanshard Needle asking for this ending to refresh into a coming. This cellular verbing will burst and spill across the latitude, erasing etchings of geography, nation, province, territory, and treaty so as to divine the directions between this world and the Fourth, knowing upwards and downwards to be as valid a mapped direction as north and south are. This mutating unlanguage will ride the crest of coming and of ending down into the confluence of the Rockies trench. Here I'll lick into the Selkirk Mountain and wormhole home too. The rivers will all sing their Spring songs, weary from telling their Winter stories, from ktunaxa to kináksisahtai to miscousipiy to zaageeng to amiskwasîpi to kaniatarowanenneh—this choir will be a jingle dress dancing with the chinook of all-direction in the snuffing chime of all-medicine. manitowapow will beat its Two-Spirit drumming, from middle point, the belly button and first mouth of origins. The longitude of this noun we call a world, on the plane we call Earth—the flatness of this mapping—we will crack into Vs like waciy and live in all-way, upside down and right side up again, queered, aslant, widening. This blast of breath will be brought back by reverbing kickback, snapped back into our dimensionality—and just like that, the end will end its ending, and we will have survived again, surfing the tin lid of a junk-yard can.

MUCH OF MY WORK in life—but this has been exacerbated during COVID—is that of an alleviator. Like a salve, I spread myself across my kin and their injurious scars. I find myself to be a pain eater; I swallow whole wounds and dissolve them in the pit. My gift, if not my role, is that of a listener, advice giver, holder. I will ask you how you are, that light touch of finger to bicep, the invitation to spill, overflow. I will look you directly in the eye, cock my head from time to time, and eat language, crunch syllables and syllabic, chew through comma and end-stop, crush synecdoche, and lap up metaphor. You will tell me what ails you and I will leach the sweat from your skin into mine, wholly pluck from you thorn and stone that has edged into your spirit-skin, and swallow.

You will leave lighter, and I will move inward, animate organ, place my eyes into my intestines, dissolve pain into mineral and enzyme, and defecate it in the morning.

This is an act of reciprocity I enact with kin. These many months have been a gluttony of pain eating—from witnessing Black and Indigenous death, the collapse of our social and intimacy networks, the skyrocketing of COVID cases and negligence, the isolation and loneliness of monotonous being, the glare of pixel and snowfall. My stomach swelled into a junkyard, the pain I ate a boulder in the gut. I dragged this weight of hurt across the floor to pour myself a glass of water, then shouldered myself along the wall to return to my bed. I pummelled my most intimate flora with the fatty gels of this eating and made a graveyard of a flower bed.

I think this digestive act is a technique that comes from proximity: my ability to witness those who showcase how their bodies morphed into malfunction, albeit temporarily. I hold and make space for their molasses confessions, as I am malleable and full of grit. Perhaps pimatisowin is a kin of pihtâkosiwin, which is the act of being heard, a voiced sound—here pihtâkiyaw, to move inside the body; inwardly I enact pihtâkosiwak, the chant. When you speak, I peek from behind my duodenum; this is where my head is. Like a constellation, the walls of this well are as alit as syrup skies, glucagon, amylase. I too am a wildness, like the tongue, and I have sprouted into a husk in this gestational entrapment. At first, the chant I heard was, "Baby, can you hear me now? The chains are locked and tied across the door," ringing from the ampulla. I stretched nerves in those days to feel for the biliary tree, and peeked into the hollowness of my cavernous self, the ducts of these travails—and paid homage to the sibling lost there to a Western diet, heavy with stone. I pulled through his star mouth, "Baby, sing with me somehow." Those were days when I could feel only the chasm of the missing within me, baby fingering the ducts, holding on to this sludge of harm, until I too became a monstrous swelling. Now pihtâkosiwak sounds like nimôsom's singing alone in that ratty shack, the smell of stale Budweiser wafting in the air, the yellowing of cigarettes a wallpaper of its own, Ernest Monias and Don Williams the hymns of his sanctimony. When I chew lipid and protein—meaning loss and pain—I chant into song, sâh-sainiskênin kîhtwâm wâh-wîhtamawin wiya ohci ninpîkotêhêh: "so full of love and pretty dreams that two should share." This eating and defecating, like maskwa and his grease, enriches the gap between vibrato tongue and bound mouths. Then omôsi-htawin, pihtâkoyaweksawew, is churned into enrichment and betterment through omow; is that why these words share a prefix with omôsom? Or is my biliary tree like the Grandfather Tree, white spruce, in Cochrane? This caretaker of the infant trees, older than anthem and country, and his children hold the soil and prevent erosion—tree full of medicine, tree full of flight, bark and wood a tool transforming into canoe, resin a chewing rein, shoot tip a citrine vitamin. nimôsom posits himself in the pancreas, and as I chew, I churn worlds for you and me; as I hold against petrification, I gift the grasslands a cavalcade of birthing.

ONE OF THE DEATHS I will mourn most from this pandemic is the slow, necrotic wilting of touch. I witness how we have consciously and unconsciously entirely shifted our social dynamics as a species who, formerly, largely engaged with each other through this sense. But this death, I hope, contains potential for revival.

I am with one of my most beloved and trusted kin, both a best friend and a former long-term partner; we know each other in a holistic and whole way. We are in my temporary home after I have won a literary prize. We are celebrating with champagne and reminiscing about our contributions to my novel *Jonny Appleseed*—me as writer, and he as someone who read the earliest drafts of chapters at his kitchen table. We are laughing, crying, and cheering in unison. And yet we are on opposite sides of the room, the space between us like an expansive berth. Another dear kin of mine joins later, we three having bubbled together, and partakes in the celebration. While we converse, I take note of where we stand in the room. Where once we would have been sitting together, gleefully buckling kneecaps on the couch, we are now in carefully tiered proximity to one another. One sits in the couch looking into the kitchen, another sits in the kitchen on a stool, and I am behind the kitchen sink. We are enjoying one another's company, but it saddens me to see that our usual intimacy through proximity and touch has completely disintegrated. None of us made the announcement that we would keep our distance within the home, and yet we have entered the code of our pandemic guidelines into our social codex even in this space where we have consented to the bubble of our shared risk.

I mourn most intensely the death of the hug.

This phenomenon of mourning is akin to the psychosensual—the loss of a pleasure that has been ingrained in us as normal, for surely it is; the intimacy of touch in all its connotations: hug, handshake, bumps, knees touching, hand holding, arm brushes. Its loss is a major hindrance to our well-being in that a single touch is now expanded into extreme pleasure, endorphin crescendo, highs of reassurance meeting the deep valley of remembrance. In contrast, when I successfully complete this book, the excellence of this accomplishment meets the solitude of closing my laptop. I turn to find myself sitting in an empty room, the dim light of fluorescence casting a shadowed audience and the sound of cricket and frog croak outside my window. My psychosomatic response acts as a deterrent: when I notice how severely alone I am, my joy is archived as historical even in the moment when it is meant to gurgle and ripple through the remainder of my time within it. What does it mean when joy is pocketed as historical in the very moment it is presented into your cupped hands? What does it mean when pimatisowin, the act of living, is immediately shelved into a past tense rather than becoming an ongoing series of unfolding events? This sensation is akin to how it feels to be and embody Two-Spiritedness, in that the moments in which I achieve something are already displaced and ghosted into a past tense that will forever place its possessive apostrophe before my name and being—it will claim me but distance itself from the wingspan of my grasp; and I will always be unable to claim or regale myself within its decor, its pinnings. Now living has become a series of hauntings, poltergeists, revenants that flock to the entrances to my ceremonial spaces and enter without regard or invitation. And when I say joy, I really mean *joyed*; and when I say living, I mean having *lived*.

There is no present within a pandemic, there is only ever a coming that is beyond the grasp of flight or feel, and is a conjunction with ending, with the past that is too amiable, too pliable, and dead-mounds into brittle medicine, thirsting starvation. My psycho-well-being is somatic as I process this continual undoing and unbuttoning of being. I am never fully embodied; rather, I exist like static, dazzling but frizzling into airwaves and light speeds that blink into disappearance. This very serious undoing is a mode of pimatisowin that now has been normalized for me, a queer Indigenous person living in this nation-state we now refer to as Canada. How insidiously genocidal, I ought to think, to be living within an unfolding of bio-organic death inside a history of continual pandemics. What means lonely, what means isolation, when one has continually been deterred in this modality of being? What means alone when the vowel within this word, *a*, which too denotes embodiment and being, is spliced but tethered to its suffix, *lone*?

Where do I exist within this canyon and canon of conjecture and connectivity? I feel as if I don't and never have. And yet, within this momentous history, I am struggling to hold together the embodied and the disembodied. The price paid is the root of this equation: body. I need to, and must, exist beyond the limited scope of such a noun. I need to, and must, exist beyond the constriction of Western linguistics.

NIMICISOWIN, NIMICIMEW, NIMICIMOHIW—I am eating, I am holding, I am stuck. Perhaps this is my physical chant as a whole being, instead of a pancreas. Perhaps I return to the midpoint. We are in Golden, British Columbia, at the Trapper's Haven cabin atop the hills. You are in the kitchen chopping onion. Your hair is a golden halo in this Ktunaxa light, the sun just setting beneath the Kootenay. Your chest is backlit from the light on the stove. You are braising chicken. You are preparing for us the food from your childhood home, Senegal. Wearing nothing but a yellow Speedo, you cook like the aunties in my family do, against flaring heat on bare skin—albeit pectoral here, not voluptuous breast. Grease splatters on your thigh, and I watch it dew from coarse leg hair.

I am writing this chapter, and as you look back at me, I smile up at you. I have found a reprieve here, in the mountains, atop this hill in Golden, in this temporary home we'll share for the next six days. I have found safety after the risk we took to fly you here from Toronto, under the surveillance of social media, amongst the rising third wave; we have carefully calculated the risk, cutting off contact to all our kin for the sake of this trial. I have asked myself: In this risky endeavour, where we are told it is a wild act to think of being together across province and sovereign nations, what if we were not to do so? What type of risk are we furthering for ourselves then? As queer folks, risk is something we're already attuned to. But in the height of COVID-19, when we are starved entirely of intimacy, care, touch, and love—will we flee, in turn, into extreme anonymity and perhaps enact riskier behaviours within this pandemic? We're overloaded with social interactions in the virtual, but what of the body and its needs? What does risk mean, when we risk ourselves too, in this isolation?

You turn around, a plate in each hand. Yassa chicken and broken rice are placed in front of me, and we eat. And as we enjoy this meal, we stare out onto a hill that wants to be a mountain, the sun now resting in the bosom of the rock face, and I see that it is not only we who are sharing this feast. Grass sprouts back up, flowers curl into themselves, rocks sigh in the cooling of eve. In your perseverance amongst grease splatter and elemental burn, you remain animate for the sake of our continuation—nutritional and intimate and alive. That's when I know that I am not the only one eating, that I am not singular in this widespread shared intimacy, that as I eat, so too does the land—that as I chew death, askîy spews life, askîy asahkêskiw.

I am never alone in this momentous feasting.

The land is eating pain too.

IT'S JULY 2021, and I am at Prince's Island Park in Calgary, Alberta. The Every Child Matters vigil is going on, to mark the bodies of the children being found on the sites of residential schools. This ceremony is being held instead of cancelling the annual national holiday that is Canada Day. I am weary, for I have witnessed far too many deaths already. I am with a Dene friend, and we have decided that today we will not allow any whiteness in our proximities. We are wearing our orange shirts—the symbol of the missing children—to the park.

We walk from Kensington along the river. There is a heat wave in the province, and the sun bears down on us with teeth clamped around our limbs like a rez dog in heat. There is no reprieve but for the Bow River. We stop along an inlet—but here we find the water polluted by Canadian nationalists in their grotesque red-and-white attire. We dip our toes into the cool water, eyes darting from side to side, alert for danger or approach. If our beads and skin are not a dead giveaway, the orange is a homing device upon our bodies. Yet we want this release. We push into the river, we splash our faces with the cool mountain water, we wade deeper until our pelvic bones release from their rigidity and our bodies are cooled, relaxed. My hair is in a tight braid, one my friend has done for me. "It ain't no powwow braid, but it'll do," she noted earlier, bursting into laughter in her tiny apartment. We push our heads

and hair into the water, throw it back like a horse's mane, and
spark joy in the current of the riverbody; our glasses have
fallen into the water, and we are blind and blinded by sun and
whiteness alike.

We find our glasses and continue to the park. We hear the
drums, the sound of music, the laughter of aunties as their
throats strain from the intensity. When we reach the vigil, we
come upon the final song of the day. It is a round dance and
the two of us have not danced, hardly touched, for some
eighteen months. The drummers thank everyone and ask us
to round-dance this final song if we are comfortable doing
so. We succumb—now double vaccinated but still shying
away from the intimacy of touch. We join hands, my Dene
friend and I, her hand in mine moist to the touch, warm and
pulsing the rhythm of blood, and we look at one another,
eyes flaring like sun dogs, yet as gentle as dancing sky. The
feel of skin is a foreign invitation—and yet, familiar. Our
eyes divine into wells.

As we look up together, we see that hundreds of people have
joined us, forming four circles entwining into one another. This
is the largest round dance I have ever seen. And now we move
to a five-minute song, the rounds of the drum intensifying our
steps, as if a stethoscope is placed upon our chests, matching
beats. We look at one another here at the end of the end, or
perhaps a new beginning, and cry. We sob for the children, we
sob for touch, we sob for this reunion—not only of those of us
here now, but of community. We are outpouring a reservoir of

pain that we lapped up, from puddle to alleyway to great lake—
by which I mean, we ate pain from those we loved, and have
known, and have seen. And here it pours out like a great storm,
upon the sunniest day. We pound into ground, barefoot and
thrumming, until we ourselves become woodwind, until we
ourselves become drum. And again, I see that it is not we who
are eating; rather, it is we who are feeding. This land upon which
we are guest echoes our Morsing, and says to us: pimatisowin,
pimatisowin, pimatisowin!

And when I wake, I wane renewed.

Yet here I am, awake still.

TO END, LET ME start at the beginning. To find joy, I must find
its birthing:

nitôsimiskwêm entered the world through a tear—nisîmis
bore her through a gash in her gut. She burrowed into the
earth-flesh of her body and dug out a child—and named her
Akira. They had to pry her out of the bathwaters of my sister
because Akira understood the safety net of womb water: what
it held, taught, promised, and how it loved. And now she knows
her body, she owns it; she knows the truth of human engineer-
ing and the constellations of her own coding. She knows how
to rip herself away from it, too.

And she was born into a world on the cusp of revolution.

Akira enjoys the outdoors, the feel of grass, mud, rocks,
leaves, and bugs on her skin. She tries to climb trees too often,
obsesses over the wonders in the branches above, which must

feel to her like another world, the Fourth world, the home she left to visit us. Once, while she was up there, a small crow fell from the tree in our front yard, a crow still in its youth, its wings not yet fully grown. It fell from its nest and landed between two pines, squawking while its parents hovered above on the tips of trees. We found Crow in the yard, picked them up, and with a ladder we placed them back into their nest. This was how nitôsimiskwêm discovered Crow.

Crow fell again, and despite all our attempts to keep Crow alive, feed them bread, defend the pines from cats and other prey—despite all our efforts, Crow eventually died between those pines. We dug up the earth in our backyard and buried Crow there. nôhtâwiy cracked open a cigarette and we blanketed Crow in tobacco, said a prayer, closed the casket of mud atop them, and sat down, quiet, sullen, contemplative on our back patio. Crow's parents and kin flocked to the burial site, where they cawed a cacophonous cry, their squawks like the throbbing of a circle of drummers—all singing songs of pain. nitôsimiskwêm sat with us, laughing, looking up into the sky, surveying the limbs of boughs that vibrated from the weight of birds, calling the crows "beads." While she laughed, we thought about the root of those crows' cries—their baby was dead. I couldn't do anything else in that moment but clutch nitôsimiskwêm and apologize, say kisâkihitin, you too are my relation, and we remember too damn much.

Now we play together, chasing each other around the yard, nipping at one another like coyotes, wrestling cubs in the grass.

We regress into a feral state, a natural stance, a loving share; like Crow, we caw together, saying kisâkihitin, we're making it in the world. Our kisses and bear hugs are promises to continue. Eventually, tired, nitôsimiskwêm and I lie in the grass, calling those crows beads instead of birds.

What does it mean to call a bird a bead? What language does she speak, and what authority do I have to correct her? She owns her stories as much as she owns her body. Her tongue is ceremonial; she honours Crow too, in her own way, gifts them a story through tradition, gives them the name of the bead that sits on her moccasin. Both of us lie here, the weight of her body pressing into mine, the low thrum of her breath pooling into the hollow in my chest, staring up at the Manitoban sky, the sun its own type of tear. This, I think, must be what sovereignty feels like.

This, I think, must be what futurity looks like.

This, right here, is a beginning.

NOTES

Sources and references consulted or quoted are as follows:

"Who Names the Rez Dog *Rez*?"

A version of this essay was previously published in *The Malahat Review* 210 (2020). It won *The Malahat Review* Open Season Award for Non-Fiction, 2020; and a National Magazine Award for Personal Journalism, 2021.

Vuong, Ocean. *On Earth We're Briefly Gorgeous.* New York: Penguin Press, 2019.

Rogers, Maggie. *Heard It in a Past Life.* Debay Sounds and Capital Records, 2019.

"On Ekphrasis and Emphasis"

A version of this essay was previously published in *Canadian Art* (canadianart.ca/essays/on-ekphrasis-and-emphasis/).

Gilroy, Dan (dir). *Velvet Buzzsaw*. Netflix, 2019.

Kurelek, William. *This Is the Nemesis*. 1965.

Kurelek, William. *When We Must Say Goodbye*. 1977.

Kurelek, William. *Indian Hitchhiking from Saskatchewan Series #2*. 1974.

Monkman, Kent. *The Chase*. 2014.

Kurelek, William. *Seeing Red*. 2014.

Watts, Jon (dir). *Spider-Man: Homecoming*. Sony Pictures, 2017.

"A Geography of Queer Woundings"

A version of this essay was previously published in *Grain Magazine* 47.4 (2020).

Miller, Mac. *Circles*. REMember Music, 2020.

Catlin, George. *Dance to the Berdache*. 1830.

"The Year in Video Gaming"

A version of this essay was previously published in *Hazlitt Magazine* (hazlitt.net/feature/year-video-gaming).

Paperny, Anna Mehler. *Hello I Want to Die Please Fix Me: Depression in the First Person*. Toronto: Random House Canada, 2019.

Fortnite. Epic Games, 2017.

Fire Emblem: Three Houses. Nintendo, 2019.

Lineage II. NCSoft, 2003.

"Writing as a Rupture"

Fee, Margery. *Literary Land Claims: The 'Indian Land Question' from Pontiac's War to Attawapiskat*. Waterloo: Wilfrid Laurier UP, 2015.

Justice, Daniel Heath. *Why Indigenous Literatures Matter.* Waterloo: Wilfrid Laurier UP, 2018.

Lorde, Audre. *The Master's Tools Will Never Dismantle the Master's House.* London: Penguin Classics, 2018.

Maracle, Lee. *Memory Serves: Oratories.* Ed. Smaro Kamboureli. Edmonton: NEWest Press, 2015.

Legeune, Philippe. *On Diary.* Ed. Jeremy D. Popkin and Julie Rak, trans. Kathy Durnin. Hawai'i: U of Hawai'i P, 2009.

Saul, Joanne. *Writing the Roaming Subject: The Biotext in Canadian Literature.* Toronto: U of Toronto P, 2006.

Washuta, Elissa and Theresa Warburton. *Shapes of Native Nonfiction: Collected Essays by Contemporary Writers.* Seattle: U of Washington P, 2019.

Whitehead, Joshua. *full-metal indigiqueer.* Vancouver: Talonbooks, 2017.

Whitehead. Joshua. *Jonny Appleseed.* Vancouver: Arsenal Pulp Press, 2018.

"I Own a Body That Wants to Break"

"Creep." Radiohead. Capitol, 1993.

okpik, dg nanouk. *Corpse Whale.* Tucson: U of Arizona P, 2012.

"My Aunties Are Wolverines"

A version of this essay was previously published in *Grain Magazine* 46.5 (2019). It was shortlisted for a National Magazine Award for Personal Journalism, 2021.

Lady Gaga. "Joanne." *Joanne.* Interscope Records, 2016.

Wan, James. *The Conjuring 2.* New Line Cinema, 2016.

"Me, the Joshua Tree"

A version of this essay was previously published in *Prism International Magazine* 59.2 (2021).

Halberstam, Jack. *In a Queer Time and Place: Transgender Bodies, Subcultural Lives.* New York City: NYUP, 2005.

Lynn, Loretta. "High on a Mountain Top." *Van Lear Rose.* Interscope Records, 2004.

Parton, Dolly. "Joshua." *Joshua.* RCA Studio B, 1971.

Reiner, Rob (dir). *Stand By Me.* Columbia Pictures, 1986.

"The Pain Eater"

Excerpts from this essay were previously published in *Arc Poetry Magazine* 84 (2017).

Carlile, Brandi. "Party of One." *By the Way, I Forgive You.* Elektra Records, 2018.

The Highwomen. *The Highwomen.* Elektra Records, 2019.

St. Marie, Buffy. "Helpless." *She Used to Wanna Be a Ballerina.* Vanguard, 1971.

St. Marie, Buffy. "Take My Hand for Awhile." *I'm Gonna Be a Country Girl Again.* Vanguard, 1968.

ACKNOWLEDGEMENTS

YOU ASKED ME: What is your biggest fear?

That I wake up one day on a precipice—

Like a mountain cliff?

More upon the face of grammar. And I'll be reaching for a warmth to cradle my hand as if it were a mitt. Instead, my skin will only feel the cool paper of a novel. All that will be is immeasurable dearth. And me, anchored to a berth.

You asked me: What is your greatest joy?

That I wake up one day on a precipice—

Like a mountain cliff?

More upon the shoehorn of time. And I'll be reaching for a warmth to cradle my hand as if it were a mitt. Instead, my skin will only feel the cool paper of a novel. All that will be is immeasurable birth. And me, holding hands with mistik, which has never been a mistake.

TO SPEAK TRULY of this manuscript, I need to speak of its gambits. It nearly killed me a handful of times. I am always reaching for your fingers. What I have come to know in the writing, through all of its pained excavations, is that, alongside my search for a utopian vision on an unhinged horizon of unrealized potentiality, I look into the eyes of truth, sticky gauze and ineptitude, two black holes staring out from a socket sunk deep into a skull-land. Here I contemplate the prairies of the *now*, a broken treaty swinging on a sawed-off jaw. I find there a molar within which to burrow, to live out the days of this present and work myself into anotherness—which may not be a day nor a tomorrow, but a moment in which to witness the lavishness of this *now* even as it perverts, foregrounded against a doomed backdrop. A *now* that is, and has been, forever lit by the lanterns of temporality, a becoming and an oncoming. I find solace in knowing I'm quilted by eternity. I would be happy to rest there, even if for a minute, before unsheathing into the changeling I've come to know myself to be.

There are many thanks to make for the creation of these stories:

To those who harmed me, I do forgive and thank you.

To those I've harmed, I hope you find that place within you, too.

To The Canada Council for the Arts, Calgary Development for the Arts, the RBC Taylor Prize Emerging Mentorship

Program, and the Alberta Foundation for the Arts for your financial aid in the research and writing of this book.

To Writing-on-Stone, Head-Smashed-In, the Dover Hills, the Bow River, the Red River, Narcisse Snake Dens, Lake Winnipeg, and all of Treaty 7 and 1 for your gifting me of homes; and to the ancestors who dwell, move upon, and mentor on these lands.

To *EVENT Magazine, Prism International, The Malahat Review, Grain Magazine, ARC Magazine*, CBC Books and Arts for giving several of these essays their first groundings.

To Dr. Derritt Mason, Dr. Rain Prud'homme Cranford, Dr. Larissa Lai, Dr. Daniel Heath Justice, and Dr. Aubrey Hanson for your critiques, feedback, encouragement, and unwavering guidance throughout the process of creating this book in its progenitor as a doctoral dissertation.

To *Fluidfest* and all of the performers who undertook and transformed some of these essays into grand gestures of movement, music, and art.

To Stephanie Sinclair for being the most stalwart and supportive person in and of my writing.

To Lynn Henry for taking this flooding and cupping it with such grace that it became a manageable dam.

To Bernt for your care, always, seeding terrarium. What a blessing to find you, again and again.

To Chief and Dirk for sniffing out the days when your lapping was a necessary enmeshment.

To Kawennáhere for changing my life forever and showing me the power of story.

To Darren, for your boundless kindness, humour, and grace—I hope everyone can see the invisible labour of being in relation. And I never forgot the lessons.

To everyone who has shown me, and each other, generosity beyond compare. I hope to share just as much with you, when you need me.

To Brandi Carlile for always meeting my grief head-on in song, tempo, and honky-tonks.

To my parents who always know how to wrench me out of the deep well that writing can ask us to fall within.

To my sisters and brothers for your laughter and oddities, an oasis in an already shimmering mirage.

To my grandmother for showing everyone in her vicinity a hulking strength that I wish you could retire, even just a little.

To Akira for placing my hands into the earth and showing me what sovereignty feels like.

To my nephew, Alex: I hope to build a patch of land so that you'll never know a sharp tendril.

And to you, I say: writing cannot always be fuelled by injury.

JOSHUA WHITEHEAD is an Oji-Cree/nehiyaw, Two-Spirit/Indigiqueer member of Peguis First Nation (Treaty 1). He is the author of the bestselling novel *Jonny Appleseed* (2018), longlisted for the Scotiabank Giller Prize, shortlisted for the Governor General's Literary Award, and winner of Canada Reads; and the poetry collection *full-metal indigiqueer* (2017), which was the winner of the Governor General's History Award for the Indigenous Arts and Stories Challenge in 2016. He is also the editor of *Love after the End: An Anthology of Two-Spirit and Indigiqueer Speculative Fiction* (2020). He recently completed a PhD in Indigenous Literatures and Cultures in the University of Calgary's English department (Treaty 7), where he teaches and writes. Joshua Whitehead lives in Calgary, Alberta.